Elizabeth Anna Sophia Dawes

The Pronunciation of Greek

With Suggestions for a Reform in Teaching that Language

Elizabeth Anna Sophia Dawes

The Pronunciation of Greek
With Suggestions for a Reform in Teaching that Language

ISBN/EAN: 9783337297053

Printed in Europe, USA, Canada, Australia, Japan

Cover: Foto ©Thomas Meinert / pixelio.de

More available books at **www.hansebooks.com**

THE

PRONUNCIATION OF GREEK

WITH

SUGGESTIONS FOR A REFORM

IN

TEACHING THAT LANGUAGE

BY

E. A. S. DAWES, M.A. (LOND.)

"Est ridiculum, ad ea, quæ habemus, nihil dicere ; quærere, quæ habere non possumus ; et de hominum memoriâ tacere, litterarum memoriam flagitare."—
CICERO, *Pro Arch.* iv. 8.

D. NUTT, LONDON

1889

THE
PRONUNCIATION OF GREEK.

THE rise of the Greek nation from its long bondage, and its rapid progress in general development, in political importance, in commerce and in education during the last fifty years, reveals an inherent tenacity and vigour of life which has scarcely ever been witnessed in any other people. The rapid means of communication has also brought Greece within easy access of Western Europe, and the once distant country is readily visited by numerous travellers, either for mere pleasure, or to study the relics which still attest the former supremacy of Greece in art and architecture. This new intercourse with a nation whose literature has had so much influence on the world at large, and is the *fons et origo* of so much of its intellectual development, has led many scholars, especially in Germany and Holland, to reconsider the question of the proper pronunciation of the language, and to study the language as at present spoken and written in Greece itself. The scholars of England can hardly be said to have fairly turned their attention to this subject. Until very lately modern Greece, its language and literature, found but little favour in the ranks of our scholars, and even to the present day there exists a remarkable ignorance among us of the progress,

A 2

improvement and multiplicity of the works which are constantly issuing from the press in Greece.

There is in England a general indifference to any modern Greek literary production, or more generally complete ignorance of the existing literature—the prevailing idea being that modern Greek is a very different language from ancient Greek, and that the present language is so debased that the ancient can hardly be recognized in it. The general use of the expression "modern Greek" has led to a deepening of this opinion, and very few of those who have spent the best years of their lives in the study of Greek at the public schools and universities have any idea of the language now spoken in the land where the great writers of Greek antiquity wrote their immortal productions; and they would be surprised if they were told that the lexicon of Liddell and Scott which they have so often used is the best for the language now spoken, some idioms and provincialisms excepted. But who can tell how many idioms and provincialisms of the best times of Attic literature are not contained in any lexicon, and perhaps are only to be found in the traditional deposits of the nation and expressed by the people now as they were thousands of years ago ? Professor Blackie, who is an exception to the general rule in this country, writes in the *Hellas* (the magazine of the Hellenic Society in Amsterdam) :—"I am constantly meeting with intelligent persons who labour under the impression that the language of Plato and S. Chrysostom is a dead language, as much as Latin and Hebrew. In an age when Greek newspapers and Greek books on a great variety of subjects are published every day, the existence of such a notion among intelligent persons is a sad sign of that 'insular ignorance' with which Professor Seeley reproached the inhabitants of this tight little island;

and it is a notion pardonable enough in the general public, as professional scholars unfortunately have done not a little to give currency to so gross a misconception. For professors and schoolmasters, and teachers of the classical languages generally, partly from their habit of devolving their living function as teachers of language on dead books, and partly from their *barbarous habit of murdering the classical tongue by Latin accentuation and English vocalization*, have taken up a position that, so far as they and their disciples are concerned, makes the living language of Greece practically dead; and so complete is this deadness, that when our young Greeklings, after it may be ten years' study of Greek in Eton or Oxford, make a tour to the land where the language is spoken, they find that scarce a sentence in their well-crammed Hellenism is understood, and forthwith, instead of blaming themselves and their teachers for their barbarous treatment of the language of the Muses, they denounce the spoken language as barbarous." This represents the prevailing opinion among us, which we trust will soon be one of the past. The term modern should no more be used as an adjective before Greek to represent the Greek of to-day, than before English or French to distinguish those languages from what they were in the fifteenth or sixteenth century. German of the present day differs more from the language of Luther than the Greek of to-day from that of classic times. No romance language approaches so near Latin as the Greek of to-day to that of Plato. The different Latin dialects, which are now classed as languages in Europe, have deviated in so many particulars from the parent tongue that the Latin scholar has to make a separate study to acquire any one of them. The Greek scholar has not this difficulty, if he wishes to read the writings of modern Greeks. He will find when he begins to study the

modern literature such a surprising resemblance as to excite his
astonishment, and to refute the ideas he may have had as to the
language being so utterly changed as to be unintelligible to the
classical scholar. On the contrary, he will make the agreeable
discovery that at first sight he can understand as easily as
classical Greek most of the well written books, and with a
few weeks' study he will be able to read the newspapers and
periodicals. The popular language, as in every country, will
offer more variety of dialectic form, and not be so readily
acquired by the classical student, but is a most interesting
philological study. The pronunciation is the principal difficulty which the Western scholar finds on his arrival in Greece,
and it is this which stands as a wall of separation between the
scholars of the West and those of Greece, and which hangs the
shroud of death around the ancient classic tongue, and brands
the Attic wit of the present day as barbaric to those who have
contented themselves with pronouncing Greek, a foreign tongue,
in the same manner as their own language.

This curious question of how a language should be pronounced
—a language which is living, which has always been spoken and
has had a continuous literature even in times when the national
life seemed almost extinct, is the one we propose to examine
briefly in the following pages :—

There can be no doubt but that in a language so widely
spoken as the Greek was about the time of the Christian era
there must have existed many dialectic forms and varieties
of pronunciation. It is not long since persons from the different
counties of England could be readily recognized by their pronunciation; some counties had more marked differences of
dialect than others, and still retain, especially among the lower
classes, many of these peculiarities of pronunciation, and also

many words and expressions peculiar to their own counties; the same may be said of most European countries. The standard of a language in form and pronunciation must be sought for among the educated and those residing in or near the centres of intellectual development, which in most cases is the capital town of the country. We may fairly assume that after the fall of Greece proper, and the rise of the Byzantine power, Constantinople with its statesmen, orators and writers, and Alexandria with its grammarians and schools of philosophy, would be centres of learning in which the Greek language was spoken and written with comparative purity. The writings of the Alexandrian grammarians attest their anxiety for the preservation of the purity of their language and the correctness of its pronunciation. We cannot suppose that Chrysostom would have gained the epithet by which he is now known had he not had a pure pronunciation and a flowing delivery.

The language continued to be spoken, studied, and written with care in Constantinople until the fall of the Byzantine empire and the capture of the city by the Turks.

After the capture of Constantinople many learned Greeks left the city and migrated into western Europe and gave an impulse to the then awakening spirit for letters. Among these men may be noted the famous Theodorus Gaza, who composed a grammar for the use of those who were studying Greek, the first two parts of which were translated by Erasmus. No one at that time thought that the writings of the ancients should be read with any other pronunciation than that which these men brought with them. Greek was then pronounced with its own living pronunciation and learned as a living language. Wherever these refugees from Constantinople taught their language they taught their own pronunciation and their pupils taught it to others, and so they read and spoke the language as a living one. It seems to be a *petitio principii* to say that this traditional pronunciation of these men was a wrong one, and yet this is the argument or statement of the opponents of the present pronunciation—the followers of the Erasmian system.

It was not till 1528 A.D. that the learned world was surprised by the theory of another pronunciation for Greek than the generally received and traditional one, when Desiderius Erasmus of Rotterdam made known his discovery in a treatise entitled " De recta latini græcique sermonis pronunciatione dialogus." The dialogue is supposed to take place between a clever Bear and a learned Lion. It is more a witty than a serious production, and which of these two Erasmus intended it to be is now difficult to assert. The clever Bear undertakes to prove to the Lion that the pronunciation in use among the Greeks of their own language is quite wrong, and that they do not know how to pronounce it, that the right pronunciation of ancient Greek had been lost in the course of time and the various transitions through which the nation had passed, and therefore it was necessary to reconstruct the pronunciation by giving to the vowels and consonants the sounds which he supposed they originally had, and suggested that the ancient Greeks had similar sounds to those in the Dutch language with a slight admixture of French and German sounds.

That Erasmus himself ever adopted the pronunciation recommended in the famous dialogue seems to be very improbable. He appears to have used the traditional pronunciation himself, and to have taught it to his students, and he begged his Greek friend Lascaris to find him a Greek as teacher, that the children might learn to pronounce properly. " Conducendus aliquis natione Græcus, licet alioquin parum eruditus, propter nativum illum ac patrium sonum, ut castigaté græca sonari discantur." And in another letter to Lascaris he says : "Meum consilium semper fuit, ut adsciceretur Græcus natus unde germanam græci sermonis pronuntiationem imbibant autores."

It seems almost incredible that, after such strongly expressed opinions in favour of the living pronunciation of Greek, Erasmus should have suddenly abandoned it for one totally different and purely artificial, which in a jocular moment he had propounded in his famous dialogue. If he did—for this point is somewhat uncertain—he does not appear to have had an immediate wide-spread influence even in his own country. In fact, the so-called Erasmian pronunciation seems to be a posthumous child, born some fifty years after the death of its reputed father. The grammatical bibliography of the latter half of the sixteenth century shows this clearly, since grammars continued to be published in which the traditional pronunciation was adopted ; and these books were used in the schools of Belgium, Holland, and Germany.

We may mention among those who continued to use the traditional pronunciation Theophilus Golius, who in 1572 published his instructions in the Greek language, for the use of the Gymnasium of Strasburg.

In the same year (1572) there issued from the press of Christopher Plantin, Antwerp, a *Lexicon Græcum et institutiones linguæ Græcæ*. In 1530 Nicolas Clenardus published his *Institutiones in linguam Græcam* at Louvain.

Afterwards he published, in 1576, at Antwerp, from the press of Plantin, his *Absolutissimæ institutiones in linguam Græcam*. In none of these is there any mention of a new pronunciation, but the rules given are according to the traditional one.

This grammar of Clenardus was in use until 1625, also in the schools of Holland, as we learn from the time-table of the schools for the year 1625, approved by the Council of Holland : " Diebus Lunæ, Martis, Jovis et Veneris hora IV. Rudimenta e grammatica Græca CLENARDI recensita *nempe doctrina de litteris*, accentum notis declinationibus atque comparationibus."

In the following year (1626) however, we find that the Erasmian pronunciation was introduced into the schools of Holland by Gerard Voss, and his book ordered to be used in the schools : 'Gerardi Jo. Vossii linguæ Græcæ rudimenta, quibus decreto ordinum Hollandiæ . . . in usum scholarum ejusdem Provinciæ."

In this book Voss explains the pronunciation according to the so-called Erasmian, and warns the pupils against that in use, that is the traditional one, and that they must not pronounce the vowels and diphthongs as they have been accustomed to, or according to the general practice.

But this system of Voss does not appear to have been introduced into the schools of Belgium, until later at least, for there and in many schools of Germany the old pronunciation continued to be used and was taught in the grammar of Jacob Gretser, professor at the University of Ingoldstadt—*Rudimenta linguæ græcæ ex primo libro institutionum Jacobi Gretseri.* Leodii. J. Ouwerk. 1637.

Thus we learn that for many years after Erasmus the old pronunciation was taught in Belgium, Holland, and Germany, and that the new pronunciation, introduced by Voss into his grammar, was not authorized to be used in Holland until ninety years after the death of Erasmus, its reputed originator.

The influence of the Erasmian theory however, from the want of proper teachers, *i.e.* Greeks for the pronunciation, and the comparative neglect into which the study of Greek fell, gradually caused the traditional pronunciation to disappear from the schools; and, in the different countries of Europe, Greek was pronounced according to the respective sounds of the language of the country in which it was taught, so that no Greek student of one country understood the Greek student of another, and a Greek could not understand any one of them. This confusion exists unto the present day, but will, we hope, by degrees disappear as scholars begin to understand more fully the present state of the Greek language and its literature, which is increasing daily in quantity and quality.

Since the end of the sixteenth century until lately, the question of the pronunciation of Greek has remained in abeyance. In England very little interest has been felt with respect to it, and therefore we shall be obliged to refer more especially to Continental writers. Professor Blackie has for some years been the champion of the traditional pronunciation, but he has found little response in these islands. A. R. Rangabé, the veteran scholar of Greece, published his pamphlet, *Die Aussprache des Griechischen* in 1861, and a second edition in 1888. Dr. Engel, of Berlin, published an interesting volume in 1887, *Die Aussprache des Griechischen*. These are the principal defendants of the traditional pronunciation. There has just appeared at Athens a work by Th. Demetrakopoulos, which we have not yet seen, but which appears from a review in the "ʹΕστία" to treat this question very exhaustively.

In 1869 and 1870 Professor Blass, of Kiel, came forward as defendant of the Erasmian views, and last year a third and enlarged edition of his work appeared. This, coming at a time when the question of Greek pronunciation is beginning to be reconsidered, has attracted some attention. Professor

Zacher also published a pamphlet last year in support of the same views. Professor Blass's book is perhaps the most important defence of the Erasmian theory that has appeared since the sixteenth century. He examines carefully all the vowel sounds and diphthongs, and with great critical acumen supports his views from various authors and inscriptions, still for the most part he seems to fail to prove that the Greeks ever pronounced according to the Erasmian system.

When the Erasmians change in the pronunciation nearly all that has been received as traditional, they must not only endeavour to prove in detail those things which have not been disputed by those who favour the traditional pronunciation, and questions which were admitted before the time of Erasmus, but they must prove that the bold so-called restorations which they introduce, did really exist in the ancient pronunciation. As yet, however, they have not succeeded in proving this in any of their writings that have appeared from the time of Erasmus to the present day. They cannot show conclusively that the traditional pronunciation is wrong and their own theory right, and that for the simple reason that the former is the true one, handed down from generation to generation and supported by the Greek grammarians, the immediate descendants of the ancient Greeks, and thus resting on an historical basis, whilst the most important arguments of the Erasmians are generally based on mere conjectures, and not on clear and indisputable proofs. They have only invented a barbarous-sounding pronunciation which no such refined and æsthetic nation as the Greek could ever have used.

That the present pronunciation among the Greeks is in every respect the same as it was in the days of Pericles the Reuchlinians do not presume to assert, but they admit that possibly the long and short vowels were distinguished, and that the sounds of η, υ, and the diphthong οι differed in some degree from that of ι. They are, however, of opinion that the present pronunciation is identical with that in use at the beginning of the Christian era, and that of Plutarch and the Evangelists.

In the case of all languages the living traditional pronunciation is accepted as the one to be adopted, and this is what we ask for the Greek language, which more than any other European language has retained a pronunciation that can be traced back at least about two thousand years. The proofs of this are to be found in inscriptions, and in transcriptions from Greek into Latin, and Latin into Greek, and in the remarks of the grammarians; these last, however, must be used with caution.

The chief controversy between the Erasmians and Reuchlinians turns on the pronunciation of the diphthongs, except ου, and a few of the vowels and consonants. The majority of the vowels and consonants are pronounced in the same manner by both parties, α, ε, ι, ο, ου (the latter pronounced as oo in boot); γ, κ, λ, μ, ν, ξ, ϖ, ρ, φ, τ, χ, ψ are generally admitted to have retained their ancient sounds in the modern Greek pronunciation, the same is admitted with respect to δ, θ, σ, and ντ by all Erasmians who have studied the question scientifically. The diversity of opinion is chiefly confined to the letters η, υ, ω; αι, ει, οι, αυ, ευ, υι; β, ζ and μπ.

In consequence of the different pronunciation of the letter η the parties were named Itacists and Etacists. The former term was given to the Reuchlinians, who pronounce the η as the Greek iota or the English e in "be;" the latter to the

Erasmians, who pronounce the η as ey in they, or as the
German e. The sound of η however does not indicate the
chief difference, as most Reuchlinians are willing to concede
that in the classical period there may have been a slight
distinction between the sound of ι and η. The real crux is
the pronunciation of the diphthongs, which affects the sound
of the language much more than that of the single letter η.

The German pronunciation of Greek is the only one which
resembles the Erasmian, and therefore we shall refer principally
to this in the following pages. The English pronunciation is
admitted not to be the correct one by all scholars, and has
no claim to be called Erasmian.

The following arrangement of the letters will show clearly
the divergencies of the two systems.

The letters a, ε, ι, κ, λ, μ, ν, ξ, o, π, ρ, τ, φ, χ, ψ, and the
diphthong ου, are pronounced alike by both parties. The other
letters as follows:—

ERASMIAN.	REUCHLINIAN.
β = German and English b	= w in ewig ; v in ever.
γ = German and English g	= German j or English y before ε, η, ι, υ; before other vowels a sound between g and h—German g in tag.
δ = German or English d	= English th in then.
ζ = German z in zeit	= English z in zebra.
η = German e=English ay in day	= German i, or English e in be.
θ = German or English t	= English th in thin.
σ = German soft s if initial ; if medial or final, hard s	= hard s ; before β, γ, δ, μ, soft s.
υ = German ü, or French u	= German i, or English e in be.
ω = long ō	= as o in hope, but very little difference between it and o.
αι = German ai in kaiser ; English i in tiger	= German e ; English ey in day.
ει = the same as αι	= German i ; English e in be.

ERASMIAN.   REUCHLINIAN.

οι = German *eu* in *heu* ; English
    oy in boy   = German *i* ; English *e* in be.

υι = German *ü* ; French *u*   = German *i* ; English *e* in be.

αυ = German *au* in Frau ; English⎫ = ⎧English *af* ; but before medials,
    ow in how   ⎭ ⎩liquids, and vowels, *av*.

ευ = German *eu* in *heu* ; English⎫ = ⎧English *ef* ; but before medials,
    oy in boy   ⎭ ⎩liquids and vowels, *ev*.

ηυ = The same as ευ   = English *ēv* in *evening*.

One of the principal objections brought forward by the Erasmians, or quasi-Erasmians, who use the pronunciation of their own language for Greek is the frequency of the iota sound (expressed as our *e* in " be ") in the traditional Greek pronunciation—the Iotacism or Itacism. This repetition of the same vowel sound for different vowels or combination of vowels is not peculiar to Greek, but may be found in most languages. The Greek language, far from exceeding all others in the repetition of the same sound when three vowels and three diphthongs are pronounced as iota, has been shown to have fewer *ē* sounds than Latin when pronounced by Italians—and than other languages have other predominating vowel sounds. Rangabè and Dr. Engel have carefully counted these sounds, and furnished us with interesting results, showing that the iota sound in the traditional pronunciation is not in excess of some other vowels in other languages.

In Cicero's First Oration against Catiline (ch. i.), and in *Pro Milone* (ch. i.), out of 1,115 vowels 311 are *i* sounds, or 27·8 per cent.

In the beginning of Sallust's *Catiline*, of 470 vowels 139 are *i* sounds—29·5 per cent.

In Cæsar's *Bellum Civile* (ch. xxi. and half of xxii.) 501 vowels—152 *i* sounds—30·3 per cent.

In Tacitus' *Germania* (chaps. vi. and vii.) 744 vowels—186 *i* sounds—25 per cent. Dr. Engel has counted and found :
In Cicero's *De Oratore*, book i. chaps. i. and ii., 1,239 vowels —347 *i* sounds—28 per cent. ; book ii. chap. i., 888 vowels— 233 *i* sounds—26·2 per cent. ; book iii. chaps. i. and ii., 1,344 vowels—387 *i* sounds—28·7 per cent. In Cæsar's *Bellum Gall.*, book i. chaps. i. and ii., 765 vowels— 223 *i* sounds—29·1 per cent. ; book ii. chaps. i. and ii., 502 vowels—135 *i* sounds—26·8 per cent.

Even in Plautus, who so often employs *u* for *i*, in act i. of the *Trinummus*, 1,170 vowels—304 *i* sounds—25·9 per cent.

The result of these calculations is that out of 8,738 vowels in Latin, 2,417 are *i* sounds, or 27·6 per cent.

Such words as the following show the frequency of the *i* sound—inimicitiis, inimicissimis, didicisti, dixisti, tristitiis, divitiis, and very many others.

Also such verses as—

" Dic mihi, quid feci, nisi non sapienter amavi ? "

" Nec tu linigeram fieri quid possit ad Isim."

" Proveniant medii sic mihi sæpe dies."

" Quid tibi vis, mulier, nigris dignissima barris ? "

" Quid fles, Asterie, quem tibi candidi
Primo restituent vere Favonii."

" Quod si me lyricis vatibus inseris, sublimis feriam vertice sidera."

" Sin aliter es, inimici atque irati tibi."

From ancient Greek read with the traditional pronunciation we get the following results : *i.e.* ι, η, (ῃ), ει, οι, υ, υι, pronounced as our *ē* in " be " as follows :—

Xenophon *Anabasis*, book i. chap. i. §§ 1-8, 832 vowels—222 *ē* sounds—26·6 per cent.

Thucydides, *Peloponnesian War*, book i. chaps. i. and ii., and book ii. chap. liv., 1,152 vowels—303 ē sounds—26·9 per cent.

Plato's *Apology of Socrates*, i. and ii.; *Phædo*, i.; *Sophist*, i., 2,128 vowels—551 *e* sounds—25·8 per cent.

Demosthenes' *De Pace* (§§ 1-6), 722 vowels—175 ē sounds— 24·2 per cent.

Lysias' *Speech against Nicomachus* (§§ 1-6), 817 vowels—216 ē sounds—26·4 per cent.

Lucian's *Somnium*, the first fifty-three lines, 1,007 vowels —270 ē sounds—26·8 per cent.

Sophocles, *Ajax*, the first 100 lines, 1,210 vowels—317 ē sounds—26·4 per cent.

Æschylus, the *Persæ*, lines 353-432, 960 vowels—258 ē sounds—26·8 per cent.

The total result of the above countings shows that the ē sound occurs in ancient Greek, read according to the traditional pronunciation (so called modern Greek pronunciation) 2,312 times out of 8,791 vowels, or 26·2 per cent. Thus we may say that, whilst the *e* sound occurs 26 times, other vowels occur 74 times.

The following table may show the relative frequency of particular vowels more clearly :—

The frequency of the *e* sound in German 42·8 per cent.
,, ,, ,, *e* ,, French 36·3 ,,
,, ,, ,, *i* ,, Latin 27·6 ,,
,, ,, ,, ι in Ancient Greek
with the traditional pronunciation 26·2 per cent.

Thus clearly showing that the redundancy of the iota sound pronounced as our *e* in be, is less than that of other vowel sounds in other languages, and therefore the objection so often and so thoughtlessly made as to the frequency of the *e* sound

B

loses its force as soon as it is investigated with a certain amount of accuracy.

Such words as τῆς ἀληθηίης = tēs ălĕthḗēs, τῆς ὑγιείης = tēs ēgēēs have been cited against the traditional pronunciation ; these, however, happen to be forms of the Ionic dialect, but do these sound any better with the Erasmian or English pronunciation ? There are in all languages some not very pleasing sounds, but the general euphony of a language is not judged by its exceptions.

There is nothing to lead us to suppose that the Greek language differed, or differs, from others in having several signs to represent the same sound, and that very early the one sound of ē in be, the iota sound, was expressed by several signs as it is at present by the six following : ι, η, υ, ει, οι, υι, which are all now pronounced in most cases exactly alike.

In English the same sound is frequently expressed by several signs as the e sound in the following words :—i (big, bitch) ; y (lynx) ; e (be) ; ea (beach) ; ee (bee, see) ; ei (ceiling) ; ey (key) ; ie (field) ; æ (Æneas) ; œ˙(Eubœa) ; ui (biscuit).

In German the e sound is expressed by i, ie, ich ; in ihr, sie, fliehen.

In French the sound of our a in mate, with but very slight ·modifications from the lips of those who try to make them, but wholly unnoticed in general reading and conversation, may be expressed by the following signs :—é, è, ê, et, êt, est, ei, ai, ès, ais, ait, aient. The o sound can be written : o, ó, os, ot, ots, ôt, ôts, ost, au, aux, cau, caux, aut, auts, aud, auds, oz, auz.

These examples are sufficient to show, that the Greeks are by no means isolated in having several signs to express one sound and that the argument of the Erasmians against the traditional pronunciation of ι, υ, η, ει, οι, υι, can have but little weight, especially as we know they were pronounced as they are now before the Christian era.

Objections are also made to the *harsh* sounds in such words as εὔκολος=efkolos and εὔστρωτος = éfstrotos, and yet Erasmians do not complain of words like ἀστειεύομαι pronounced in German ástei-eúomai, English astī-uomī; or αἰτεῖται, German aitcitai, English ītītī; or οἱ εὔῤῥωστοι υἱοί, German heu eurosteu üeu, English hoy urōstoy whyoy; εὐειδεῖς, German eucidcis, English uīdīs. To those who speak Greek the Erasmian pronunciation of these and such words appears most harsh and unpleasant, whereas with the traditional pronunciation they flow easily and are euphonious.

The Erasmians assert that the ancient Greeks must have originally tried to represent the sounds of their language by the letters of their alphabet, and say that the simple and natural rule, "Write as you speak," is never transgressed without some good reason. In other words the primitive alphabet must have been phonetic. The Greeks however borrowed their alphabet from the Phœnicians, and adapted it as well as possible to represent the sounds of their own language approximately; after some considerable time they added a few signs of their own to express some sounds more correctly, we may suppose.

But neither modern nor ancient alphabets appear to be phonetic but in a very limited sense. Two of the oldest we know are the Cretan and Cyprian, which are far from being phonetic, if being phonetic means having a separate sign for each separate sound.

The Cretan has eighteen letters and the Cyprian only fifteen, and consequently it is most likely that the same sign frequently represented different sounds.

The Cyprian alphabet does not distinguish the tenues, mediæ or aspiratæ, and has no spiritus asper. Besides the five vowel sounds *a, e, i, o, y*, there are only ten consonants, *k, t, p, l, r, n, m, j, v, z, x*, and yet with this paucity of signs it was able to express all that was necessary. It is a well-known fact that ancient alphabets are generally defective, and it is only in an advanced stage of civilization that alphabets are made more phonetic.

According to Pliny and Tacitus the Greek alphabet had originally only sixteen signs (instead of the later twenty-four), according to Aristotle eighteen; we may infer therefore that the alphabet was very far from being phonetic (and yet with this meagre orthography they gave to the world the *Prometheus* of Æschylus, the *Antigone* of Sophocles, and other monuments of literary labour which have remained unsurpassed.)

In the archonship of Eukleides 403 B.C., an addition was made to the Attic alphabet. The sign *H* which had hitherto served to denote the spiritus asper, was employed to represent a long *e* sound, which implies a necessity for this; also *ει* which had before been represented by *ε*, and *ω* and *ου* which had both been represented by *o*. These additions were no doubt made on phonetic principles, and removed some of the existing deficiencies, but they were far from rendering the alphabet phonetic, that is, capable of expressing all the sounds in the language.

We may fairly, however, suppose that the historical orthography, for the most part, remained unchanged and in many cases opposed to strict phonetic laws, notwithstanding the introduction of these four new signs. There is in every country a strong conservative tendency to retain historical orthography; one generation writes as the former one has taught it to do, and does not stop to inquire whether the signs still correctly express the sounds they are supposed to represent. If grammarians and etymologists were wanting in Attica, there were priests, statesmen, and jurists who would wish to abide by the historical orthography such as they saw in their archives and in inscriptions; in a state where so much reverence was paid to the due performance of religious rites, and the maintenance of old customs, there would exist a kind of superstitious dread against changing the time-honoured spelling which their fathers and forefathers had used and handed down to them.

The Greek of the fifth century was a modern language to the people then living, and they spelt their words as they saw former generations had done. They had their Homer and Hesiod, their Alcman and Simouides as their classical writers, and probably many contemporaneous writers now unknown, which would serve as standards of orthography, and the few additional letters which had gradually grown into use and supposed to have been generally accepted about 403 B.C. would not make much alteration.

The Erasmians, however, assert that the Greek pronunciation has changed in the course of time; many are satisfied with the mere assertion, "the ancient Greeks could never have spoken as they do now." But the Reuchlinians, or defenders of the traditional pronunciation, do not deny that the pronunciation may have changed from what it was originally; they wish however to find some definition or approximation of the limit of time. To speak of original pronunciation and ancient Greeks is very indefinite, and leads us into the unknown. "Est ridiculum, ad ea, quæ habemus, nihil dicere; quærere, quæ habere non possumus; et de hominum memoriâ tacere, litterarum memoriam flagitare."

We have not sufficient data by which we can decide as to the original pronunciation, whenever that may have been, nor to make clear what it was when the Greeks adopted the Phœnician alphabet. For all practical purposes it is sufficient if we can obtain an approximate idea of what it was in the fourth and fifth century B.C.

The oldest extant documents are now thought to belong to the ninth century B.C., and it is generally believed that the Greeks adopted the Phœnician alphabet in the ninth century B.C., if not earlier (v. Hicks' *Manual of Greek Historical Inscriptions*). Thus it is possible that by the fifth or fourth the pronunciation had changed, or settled down to some kind of uniformity. Of the original pronunciation of the language we cannot know anything definite, and it is a mistake to speak of the original pronunciation, as if it must necessarily have been dentical with that of the fourth and fifth centuries B.C., an error into which the defenders of the Erasmian pronunciation at times seem to fall.

The diphthongs may have been pronounced originally as diphthongs, but it does not follow that they were thus pronounced in the classical period; indeed Zacher, a staunch Erasmian, admits that they were fast becoming monophthongs at that time, and that the general tendency of the language was to change all diphthongs into monophthongs, thus implying that a change was going on, and that the pronunciation became, so to say, fixed in the fourth and fifth centuries B.C. We need not therefore trouble ourselves about the pronunciation anterior to this period, but limit our researches to the classical and post-classical times. We shall examine this in detail when we treat of the pronunciation of the letters and different vowel-sounds.

The Erasmians admit, that in the second century A.D. the pronunciation was the same as that used by the Greeks of to-day, with the exception perhaps of the letter η. Thus during seventeen centuries, and those most troubled and disturbed, the country invaded and ravaged by the Goths, plundered by the Normans, conquered by the Latins, Constantinople taken by the Turks, destroying the centre of Hellenic culture, and scattering its learned men over Western Europe, the rule of the Turks almost crushing out the nationality, the language retained its vitality and its pronunciation. During these long and dark ages the language might well have become changed and the pronunciation wholly altered by foreign influences, yet such is its wonderful tenacity and power, that the pronunciation does not seem to have suffered, but remains as it was in the second century A.D., and even the admixture of foreign words into the written language is very few in number.

We have a very curious and interesting memorial of the year 874 A.D., which shows that at that time, more than 1,000 years ago, not only the pronunciation was the same as to-day, but that even the same grammatical errors were in use. It is an inscription on a stone slab built into the wall of the little church of Orchomenos.

Παναγήα Θεοτώκε σὺν τὸ μονογενῆ σου ἱυῷ βοήθι τοῦ σου δούλου Λέωντος βασιληκοῦ Προτωσπαθαρίου κὲ ἐπὶ τὸν οἰκηακῶν σὺν τῖ συνεύνῳ κὲ τῦς φιλτάτυς τέκνυς αὐτοῦ, τοῦ ἐκ πόθου καὶ πήστεος μεγίστις ἀνακτίσαντος τὸν σὸν ἅγιων ναὸν. 'Αμήν.

Here we have η = ει, η = ι, υ = οι, ο = ω and vice versâ, ιυ = υι, ε = αι, and ι = η; and even the genitive τοῦ δούλου used instead of the dative exactly as it is among the uneducated of the present day.

If then the pronunciation has remained practically unchanged
through sixteen or seventeen centuries, during which the country
has undergone so many vicissitudes, why should we suppose it
to have changed so immensely in the six or seven preceding
centuries, that is, from the fourth or fifth centuries B.C. to the
first or second A.D. ?   The Erasmians maintain that in the fifth
century B.C. the diphthongs were still pronounced as broad
dipbthongs, whereas in the first and second century A.D. they
admit they were pronounced as monophthongs.   How is it
possible, we naturally ask, that such a great change, one that
alters the whole character of the sound of the language, should
have taken place just in those six or seven centuries, when the
country enjoyed comparative peace and prosperity, and the
language reached its greatest development in the works of its
most eminent writers, orators, philosophers, and poets ?

It is possible, as we have admitted, that in the centuries
preceding the fifth B.C. the pronunciation may have changed
considerably, when the nation was still in a rude and uncivilized
state.   But even before the fifth century B.C. the Rhapsodists
by reciting the works of Homer, Hesiod, and other poets, must
have assisted to keep the pronunciation to a great extent
uniform, even in the Greek colonies and settlements far from
the mother country.

How are we to account for the great change between the
fifth and fourth centuries B.C. and the first or second A.D.,
which the Erasmians assert to have taken place ?   A change
so great, as to entirely alter its sound and make it appear
like another language, and that not a kindred one.   So much
so that a Greek of the fourth century B.C. if he were accustomed
to Erasmian pronunciation, would not have been able to
understand a Greek of the first century A.D. and could not

possibly have been understood by him.   The difficulty of re-
conciling this wonderful change is increased, when we remember,
that this was the time of the highest Greek culture and
development.   It is not our duty to solve this difficulty, it
is an assertion of the Erasmians, but assertion is no proof,
and the *onus probandi* rests with them.

The many words and proper names transcribed from Greek
into Latin and from Latin into Greek, are also some guide
to the pronunciation of ancient Greek.   Yet though they
are an undoubted aid, we must be careful how we use it,
since we are not certain how the Romans pronounced Latin.
Philologists do not perhaps differ so much about the pronunciation of Latin, but still there are considerable divergencies
of opinion, as for instance, how *c* was sounded before *e* and
i, and the correct sound of *œ* and *æ*, which were used to
represent the Greek *οι* and *αι*.

Again, Greek literature did not begin to exert its influence
on the Romans until about the second century B.C., and judging from the list of Greek words given by Oscar Weise in
his work *Die Griechischen Wörter im Latein*, we may conclude
that the majority of Greek words were introduced into Latin
about the commencement of the empire.

Livius Andronicus, a native of Tarentum, is generally considered as the first who introduced Greek poetry among the
Latins in their own language.   He had a school in Rome,
and for the benefit of his pupils translated Homer and Greek
tragedies.   The influence of Greek literature, and with it the
introduction of Greek words, increased after the taking of
Sicily and capture of Carthage and Corinth by the Romans.
By degrees the Greek language became familiar to educated

Romans, who readily used Greek words to supply the deficiencies of their own tongue, especially terms pertaining
to the arts and sciences—so that Horace could write:

> " Græcia capta ferum victorem cepit, et artes
> Intulit agresti Latio."

But during this period, even by the admission of the
Erasmians themselves, Itacism was fast establishing itself,
and thus the transcriptions of this time, would be, for them,
no trustworthy evidence of the pronunciation of the fourth
and fifth centuries B.C. Words were introduced then in different
ways as they are now when taken from one language into
another. 1. Greek words were introduced without any orthographical change, each Greek letter being represented as nearly
as possible by its corresponding Latin one, without any attention being paid to the pronunciation of the whole word,
which may have been simply expressed with a Latin pronunciation, as we do in the case of such foreign names as
Paris, Berlin, and very many others. It is important to notice
that though the Latins may have transcribed Greek words
letter for letter, they may have pronounced the words differently
from the Greeks. Thus because 'Αθῆναι and ἐκκλησία were
transcribed in Latin as Athenæ and ecclesia; and census and
Lucretius were written in Greek as κῆνσος and Λουκρήτιος,
it does not follow that $\eta = \bar{e}$ in Latin; if it does necessarily
follow that η was pronounced like Latin $\bar{e}$, then the Latin
words transcribed Fidias and Piræus for Φειδίας and Πειραιεύς
prove conclusively that the Greek $\epsilon\iota$ = Latin i, which all
Erasmians are not willing to admit.

But η is not only used to transcribe the Latin $\bar{e}$, it also
takes the place of the Latin i. Polybius in the second century

B.C. writes Σκηπίων for Scipio, and Plutarch writes Παλήλια
for Palilia, and Σερουήλιος for Servilius.   These examples,
though they do not afford us any correct clue to the manner
in which the Latins pronounced the words, yet indicate that
η had a sound which fluctuated between e and i in Latin,
with perhaps a greater resemblance to the latter.

Secondly, some change was made in the spelling of the
word to represent more clearly the Greek pronunciation; these
may assist us considerably in judging of the reciprocal vowel-
sounds of the two languages.   Examples of such changes
occur in Οἰκονόμος Oeconomus; οἶστρος, oestrus; αἴνιγμα,
aenigma, and numerous other words.

Perhaps we may consider the transcription of ει by i in
Latin a more radical change, as representing the Greek
diphthong by a single vowel, as in εἰρωνεία, ironia; εἴκων,
icon; εἴδωλον, idolum.

These transcriptions, though they may not give a positive
(or absolute) clue to the ancient Greek pronunciation in consequence of our ignorance of the Latin pronunciation, yet
they give us indirect evidence through the traditional Italian
pronunciation, and in those sounds of Latin vowels about
which there exists little difference of opinion, they afford
positive evidence, as in the case of the Latin sound of i which
in Italian and all Latin languages is pronounced as our e in
be or ee in see.   This would prove that the Greek ει was
pronounced, at a very early date, like the Latin i and in
the same manner as the Greeks pronounce it now.   Although
these transcriptions cannot be used as examples of the pronunciation of the fourth and fifth centuries B.C., since few
of them go as far back as the third century B.C., yet they
prove that this pronunciation existed at that time.

It is difficult to suppose that, between the time of the
earliest of these transcriptions and the classical period, so
great an alteration can have taken place in the pronunciation
of ει as to change its sound from that of our *i* in *wine*, as
the Erasmians pronounce it, to that of our *e* in *be*.

As an example of the αι sound we may suppose such a word
as καῖσαρ, which was used by Greeks and Latins, would be
pronounced alike by both, and consequently the *ae* of the Latins,
which is now generally admitted to have been something like
our *ay* in *day*, would fairly represent the Greek sound. The
similarity of the sound of this word in the mouths of both
Greeks and Latins would be further increased if we suppose
that the present Greek sound of κ before *a*, as *kj* was then in
existence, for this palatal κ is very similar in sound to that of *c*
in Italian, which probably is the traditional sound of *c* in Latin.

Though the transcriptions may not enable us to decide
absolutely with respect to the Greek pronunciation of the
classical period, they certainly indicate with considerable
precision, that the present pronunciation of Greek does not
differ much from that at the beginning of the Christian era,
and probably for a century or two before this period.

The mistakes we find in inscriptions, when a sound has been
represented phonetically, instead of by the received orthography,
may frequently assist us in judging of the sounds represented
by the letters, which have been replaced by others through
ignorance or carelessness of the writer. Inscriptions on stone
or bronze are naturally done more slowly than writing on
papyrus, and would be in general engraven from a copy, which
in the case of public inscriptions would be written out first by
some public functionary; but still sometimes, through the want

of attention on the part of the engraver or stonemason, we find orthographical mistakes in the inscriptions, and these errors, curiously enough, often give us a clearer insight into the pronunciation than the correct writing. Such assistance as would be given to a foreigner in the case of English words like *plough* and *enough*, if he saw them written "plow" and "enuf."

When, therefore, we find on an inscription twenty examples of Ναυπακτίων written correctly, and one written ΝαϜπακτίων, we infer that the stonemason, in a moment of thoughtlessness, cut the letter Ϝ to represent the sound he usually employed in pronouncing the word; another illustration of the same sound is ῎ΕϜθετος for εὔθετος upon a Corinthian terra-cotta tablet. We have also λυπά for λοιπά, and οἱπό for ὑπό, the latter two showing clearly the similarity of sound expressed by υ and οι. Such orthographical mistakes are found in sufficient number to enable us to draw conclusions. Many of these mistakes do not appear to arise from carelessness, but from ignorance of the received spelling. Dr. Engel says that the conclusion to be drawn from inscriptions is, that, above all doubt, there is no peculiarity of the modern Greek pronunciation of the vowels, which cannot be traced back at least as far as the fourth century B.C. in one or more of the dialects of ancient Greece; whilst, on the other hand, there are no inscriptions which support the Erasmian pronunciation.

The consonnification of the ε and ι sounds (ε, αι, ι, ει, η) before a vowel is frequent in ancient Greek, and very common in modern Demotic poetry and in the language of the people. This feature does not appear to have been sufficiently noticed either by Erasmians or Reuchlinians. By consonnification of the ε and ι sounds, is meant that the ε or ι sound is pronounced like the English y, or German j, before the vowel which follows it, and to which it is joined in pronunciation. For instance, such words as παλαιός, ἀρυία, νεός, are not pronounced πα-λαι-ός, αρ-υί-α, νε-ός, but παλ-yός, ἀρυ-yά, ν'-yός in ordinary conversation and reading by the mass of the people. This is generally indicated in Demotic poetry by a curved line under the two vowels, joining them together as ἀρυία; διά in the common language is frequently written γιά, a corruption of th-ya; the iota is often very slightly heard, and the word sounds something like the German "ja."

Consonnification is known to have been very common among the Romans, and it exercised great influence on the formation of words in the Romance languages. From Quintilian we learn, that the Roman "i" and "j" had originally the same sound, and for a long time uncertainty existed as to the use of these two letters. Brachet tells us, this is why the Latin "i" in some cases has become "j" in French (or "g" soft which is the same thing). *Hierosolyma, simia, diurnus, vindemia,* have passed into *Jérusalem, singe, jour, vendage,* proving clearly that the popular pronunciation of these words was *Hjerosolyma, simja, djurnus, vindemja.* This change of the "i" into the soft sibilant "j" of the French brings two consonants together, and into a sort of collision, PIPIONEM becoming *pipjonem.* In such cases the first of the two consonants disappears; SUBJECTUS becomes *sujet;* DORSUM, *dos;* and similarly *pipjonem, tilja, raljes,* &c., become PIJONEM, TIJA, RAJES, &c., whence again come *pigeon, tige, rage,* &c.—(Brachet, *French Grammar.*)

It is also found in the German pronunciation of "Physiologie," generally sounded "Physjologie," and in all words where an "i" comes before an "o."

The principle of consonnification affords most important assistance in explaining many peculiarities of orthography found in inscriptions, and difficulties of metre. On the Gortynian inscription we find ἴωντι for ἔωντι, μωλίωντι for μωλέωντι, which orthographical difference is easily explained by admitting the consonnification of the ι and ε; the same is also found in the transcription of λεγεῶνες for "legiones."

It is this same phonetic peculiarity of the e and i sounds which appears in the warnings of the Latin grammarians against writing i for e before a vowel where consonnification assimilates the sounds of the two letters, e.g. "brattea non brattia, vinea non vinia."—(Brambach, Lateinische Orthographie, p. 133.)

On Delphic inscriptions the different forms χαλειεῖς, χαληεῖς, χαλεεῖς are found indiscriminately, which by the principle of consonnification would all be pronounced as "Chal-yis."

The simplification of αι, ει, οι before a following vowel, e.g. τέλειος, τέλεος; ἀσάλεια, ἀσάλεα is better explained by this principle than by supposing that the ει lost its ι sound and became pure ε; εἰὰν for ἐὰν; ἐννεία for ἐννέα would come under the same rule.

On an Attic inscription of 446 B.C. we find Αἰνεᾶται (C.I.A. 234) and on another of 425 B.C. Αἰνειᾶται (C.I.A. 259); here again the variance may be explained by reading ει and ε as consonant y.

The consonnification of the ε and ι sounds tends to remove many metrical difficulties which have been unsatisfactorily explained by the terms "synæresis," "crasis," &c. In fact Homer can only be properly read metrically with the traditional pronunciation; at the same time, it must be remembered that Homer was in ancient times always recited or intoned with a musical cadence, and quantities frequently have to give way to the music. The intonation of the Greek priests in reciting the prayers and reading the Scriptures in their churches, and the manner in which Mussulmans read the Koran in the mosques, may to some extent indicate the way in which Homer was recited, but to which we must add the measures of the verse to which everything else had to give way. As instances of lines which present difficulties of metrical reading, easily removed by the principle of consonnification, we may cite—

Il. i. 15, χρυσέῳ ἀνὰ σκήπτρῳ καὶ λίσσετο πάντας Ἀχαιούς.

Where χρυσέῳ must be read as a dissyllable, and is usually explained by saying that έῳ suffers synæresis, but which is really due to its being pronounced *chrys-yó*.

Il. iii. 152, δενδρέῳ ἐφεζόμενοι ὄπα λειριόεσσαν ἱεῖσι.

Where δενδρέῳ must be read *dendr-yó*.

Other lines seem to present greater difficulty, when an ει or η has to be elided or contracted with the following vowel to suit the metre, but which are easy enough and more rhythmical when the η is read as our *y*. Cases of this kind are found not only in Homer, but also in the classical poets; from Homer we may cite—

Od. iv. 352, Ἔσχον ἐπεὶ οὔ σφιν ἔρεξα τεληέσσας ἑκατόμβας.

Where ἐπεὶ οὔ must be pronounced *ep-you*.

Od. iv. 682, Ἡ εἰπέμεναι δμωῇσιν Ὀδυσσῆος θείοιο.

Ἡ εἰπέμεναι must be pronounced *yeipémenai*.
And from Sophocles—

Antig. l. 97, τοσοῦτον οὐδὲν ὥστε μὴ οὐ καλῶς θανεῖν.

Where μὴ οὐ = m'you, and also in the next example

Oed. Tyr. 13, εἴην τοιάνδε μὴ οὐ κατοικτείρων ἕδραν.

The same consonnification is sometimes found in Latin.

Virg. *Aen.* vii. 190, Aureâ percussum virgâ, versumque venenis.

„ *Ecl.* viii. 81, Uno eodemque igni ; sic nostro Daphnis amore.

Where Aureâ is pronounced *aur-ya*, and Uno eodem, *un-yodem*.

Virg. *Aen.* vi. 412, Deturbat laxatque foros, simul accipit alveo.

Where alveo is pronounced *alv-yo*.

Attention to this peculiarity of consonnification, and also to the fact that ancient Greek poetry was intoned or chanted, will remove most of the difficulties with regard to accent and metre.

We will now consider separately the letters of the alphabet and the diphthongs.

The pronunciation of the vowels *a, ε, ι, o,* has never been disputed. They are everywhere (except in England) pronounced as the Greeks pronounce them.

η.

This is the letter about which the dispute between the Erasmians and Reuchlinians has raged most fiercely, and it is in truth the one, whose probable sound in the fourth century B.C. is most difficult to determine.

It was not used as a vowel in the Attic alphabet until 403 B.C., when it was formally introduced as a long vowel ; till then it had served as the sign of the rough breathing. It is hardly to

C

be supposed that it would have been introduced into the alphabet then, if it had been pronounced exactly like long ι and could have been represented by ι, nor if it had been pronounced just like long ϵ, for then it could still have been represented by ϵ, as it had been till that time. From this it follows that η was not exactly similar in sound either to $\bar{\epsilon}$ or $\bar{\iota}$.

Blass is of opinion that the educated classes pronounced it like $\bar{\epsilon}$ till the fourth century A.D.; if this had been the case, we should find at least a few instances of its being interchanged either with ϵ or with $a\iota$ (which is allowed to have been pronounced like ϵ from the first century A.D. onwards), but such an interchange is not once found on Attic inscriptions, it is only found in Bœotia, where η was always written for $a\iota$.

Of its early tendency to become ι, or rather of the close resemblance between the sounds which were later represented by η and ι respectively, we seem to have instances in the parallel forms $\mathring{\eta}\kappa\omega$ and $\mathring{\iota}\kappa\omega$, $\epsilon\pi\mathring{\eta}\beta o\lambda o\varsigma$ and $\epsilon\pi\mathring{\iota}\beta o\lambda o\varsigma$, $\pi\acute{o}\lambda\eta o\varsigma$ and $\pi\acute{o}\lambda\iota o\varsigma$ which we find in Homer. In Attic Greek the collateral forms $\mathring{a}\mu a\xi\eta\tau\acute{o}\varsigma$ and $\mathring{a}\mu a\xi\iota\tau\acute{o}\varsigma$, $\mathring{\eta}\xi\iota\varsigma$ and $\mathring{\iota}\xi\iota\varsigma$, $\lambda\acute{a}\gamma\eta\nu o\varsigma$ and $\lambda\acute{a}\gamma\nu\nu o\varsigma$, $\tau\acute{a}\pi\eta\varsigma$ and $\tau a\pi\acute{\iota}\varsigma$ show the same resemblance between η and ι.

Line 7 from the *Batrachomyomachia*—

$$\Gamma\eta\gamma\epsilon\nu\acute{\epsilon}\omega\nu\ \mathring{a}\nu\delta\rho\hat{\omega}\nu\ \mu\iota\mu o\acute{\nu}\mu\epsilon\nu o\iota\ \mathring{\epsilon}\rho\gamma a\ \gamma\iota\gamma\acute{a}\nu\tau\omega\nu—$$

may also be cited.

The inscriptions supply us with some valuable examples of the interchange of ι and η.

In Röhl (*Inscr. gr. ant.* No. 26) we find

$$\mathring{\eta}\pi\pi o\kappa\rho\acute{a}\tau\eta\varsigma\ \text{for}\ \mathring{\iota}\pi\pi o\kappa\rho\acute{a}\tau\eta\varsigma.[1]$$

---

[1] This and several other inscriptions, which I have inserted in the text, were kindly given me by Dr. Engel of Berlin.

Ross (*Inscr. gr. erud.* No. 264) gives a Carpathian inscription of uncertain date B.C. in which ἱρώων stands for ἡρώων. An inscription from Andros (see *Le Bas Inscr.* v. 174), which dates from before the Christian era, has

πάσις ἀρετῖς for πάσης ἀρετῆς.

The most interesting examples, however, are to be found in the Gortynian inscription, which is ascribed to the fifth century B.C., and where ἀναιλίθαι stands for ἀναιλῆθαι xi. 4 (ed. Baunack Bros.) and ἐπιμολίσαι for ἐπιμολῆσαι, ix. 28. Then turning to inscriptions of the Christian era we find in Fröhner (*Inscr. grec. du Louvre*, p. 313), ὑπὲρ, εὐχῖς for εὐχῆς, and ψαλτιρίου for ψαλτηρίου on an inscription of the second century A.D., and εὐπρεπίς for εὐπρεπής on one of 313 A.D. (cf. p. 315).

Steph. Koumanoudes records in his Ἀττικαὶ ἐπιγραφαὶ ἐπιτύμβιοι (pp. 1672 ff.) the various forms Ἠπειρώτης, Ἠπηρῶτις, Ἠπιρῶτις, and Ἠλεῖα, Ἠλῆος. On an inscription from Gytheion (cf. Le Bas, 243, a) of circa 165 A.D. δινάρια is twice written for δηνάρια.

In the New Testament, also, κάμιλος for κάμηλος, ἐλάκτησε for ἐλάκτισε, ἐξυπνίσω for ἐξυπνήσω, though no doubt errors in spelling, show the prevalence of the confusion of η and ι.

Again, that η and ει were very similar in sound, is rendered highly probable by the fact that they were each held to be the representative of a long ε, and that they were interchangeable even within the limits of the same dialect. Thus we have κῆνος for κεῖνος, κλεῖς or κλῆς, κλητός or κλειτός. As even the Erasmians now admit that ει = ι from the end of the third century B.C., this interchange of η and ει shows that the three sounds η, ει, and ι were very closely, if not exactly, similar.

c 2

The most interesting of the inscriptional proofs that we have of this interchange of η and ει is that of the old Sigean inscription (C. I. G. No. 8) on which we find ἐπόεισεν for ἐπόησεν although η is used as a vowel elsewhere in the inscription. In Ross (Inscr. gr. incd. iii. 246) κῆτε occurs for κεῖται on an inscription belonging to the first century B.C.

As further examples of the interchange of η and ει in the, same dialect, we may mention the Attic imperfect ἐτίθεις, ἐτίθει, which, as Gustav Meyer says in his Greek Grammar (first edition pp. 73, 74) seems to be only orthographically different from ἐτίθης, ἐτίθη. Even in the pres. indic. we find -εις instead of -ης as the termination of the second pers. sing. So in Soph. Phil., 992 τίθεις: Soph. Ant., 403: Soph. Elect., 596, ἵεις.

The subjunctive in -ῇ is also written -ει on inscriptions of the fourth century B.C., C. I. A. 49, 10, where πραχθεῖ occurs for πραχθῇ, and C. I. A. 61, 24, where παρασκευασθεῖ occurs for -σθῇ: other examples of this can be easily found on inscriptions of the same period.

Further in C. I. A. ii. 403, 38 we have ἀνατεθηκότων (292 B.C.), whilst in C. I. A. ii. 470, 71 and 80 ἀνατεθείκασιν is written.

On an inscription of the first century B.C. we have τὴν πρεσβήαν for πρεσβείαν, and on another one of 266 B.C. (see C. I. A. ii. 332) ἀγαθῇ τύχει for τύχη, and τεῖ for τῇ.

After the first century A.D., the examples of this interchange are frequent; for instance, the inscription on the monument to the wife of Herodes Atticus has ἀναθήη (for ἀναθείη), νειόν (for νηόν), ἀτρεῖες (for ἀτρῆες) and μην (for μιν); it dates from the second century A.D. (Fröhner, No. 7). Again, on an inscription from Olbia of the time of Tiberius (Latyshev, No. 47) we read πλήονας (for πλείονας), ἐπιτάδηον (for ἐπιτάδειον), χρήας (for χρείας) and ἀσαμήωτον (for ἀσαμείωτον).

As other arguments for the similarity of η to ι and ει, we may adduce two etymologies from the *Cratylus*, the first being that of Δημήτηρ from δίδωμι and μήτηρ, the second that of Ἥρως from εἴρειν. They are obviously false, but all the plausibility they have is derived from the resemblance in sound between δη- and δι-, ηρ- and ειρ-.

So in Aristoph. *Pax*, 925, the point of the pun depends on the resemblance in sound between βοΐ and βοηθεῖν, and again, l. 928, between υΐ and ὑηνία.

In *Cratylus* 418 c. Plato says οἱ μὲν ἀρχαιότατοι ἱμέραν τὴν ἡμέραν ἐκάλουν, οἱ δὲ ἐμέραν, οἱ δὲ νῦν ἡμέραν; this remark seems to indicate that there was a slight difference between ἱμέρα and ἡμέρα, though whether it was in quality or quantity we cannot tell.

In Latin η is nearly always transcribed by ē, consequently the Erasmians say, η was pronounced like ē, that is like English "ay" in "day." Blass says that transliterations like κῆνσος for census, Λουκρήτιος, Athēnae, ecclesia are sufficient proof that η was pronounced like ē. At first sight this statement may seem perfectly correct and credible, but on closer examination, we shall find reason to take some exception to it.

Firstly, we have spoken above of the fact, that though a word may be transcribed from one language into another without any change in the spelling, it does not necessarily follow that it is pronounced alike in the two languages, cf. "Paris" in the French and English pronunciation, "Yacht" in the German and, English. The Romans would naturally transcribe the Greek η by their corresponding letter ē, even if the sounds of the two letters were not exactly similar; hence it is not a necessary consequence that "Athenæ" and Ἀθῆναι, κῆνσος and census, should have been *pronounced* exactly alike because they are *written* alike.

Secondly, η was used not only to transcribe Latin *ē*, but also Latin *i*. Thus in Plutarch we find Σερουήλιος for Servilius Παλήλια for Palilia; Polybius, who was a personal friend of Scipio's, always writes his name as Σκηπίων, Strabo and Plutarch do likewise. From this it would seem that η was an intermediate sound between Latin *ē* and *i*.

Thirdly, the pronunciation of Latin *ē* is itself uncertain. It often represented an "ei" and, on the other hand, tended to become "i," and therefore very probably closely resembled it in sound: thus we have "tristes" from "tristeis"; "Vergilius" written "Virgilius" and so on. Again, the grammarian Probus (fl. second century A.D.) warns against the wrong spellings "emago" (for imago), demidius (for dimidius); sinatus (for senatus); and Serena (for Sirena). Other grammarians recommend the spelling "filix" (for felix).

The strongest argument, however, that the Erasmians adduce to prove that η was pronounced like "ay" in "day", is the βῆ, βῆ which Cratinus uses to represent the bleating of a sheep in the well-known line :

ὁ δ' ἠλίθιος, ὥσπερ πρόβατον, βῆ βῆ λέγων βαδίζει.

the sheep, they say, cry "bay, bay" and not "bee, bee." The first objection we make to this argument is that Cratinus himself in all probability wrote βε, βε or βεε, βεε as the η was not used as a long vowel in the Attic alphabet in his time, and thus the η was introduced in the place of ε by the careless copiers of a later age, whereas it ought not, perhaps, to have been changed.

On the other hand, it is just probable that Cratinus may have used the Ionic alphabet which already possessed η as a long vowel, and have written βῆ, βῆ: in this case he may have chosen η, which from all evidence seems to have been an intermediate sound between ε and ι, as being the best adapted to express an indefinite, inarticulate animal-cry.

Finally, even if η was a distinct "ē" sound, we may remark that this same " ē " sound is found in our verb "to bleat."

The grammarian Sextus says that " the shortened form of η is ε and the lengthened form of ε is η :" here he is probably referring to the fact that etymologically η often represents the lengthening of ε as e.g. in the augments of verbs, and contractions as ἐρωτῶ, ἠρώτησα, ἐγείρω, ἤγειρα, and τείχεε, τείχη. He can hardly be referring to the pronunciation of the letters, as he did not live till the third century A.D., when there is hardly any doubt that η was generally pronounced like iota.

That η, when shortened, often becomes ε, as Sextus says, can be shown both from ancient and modern Greek, thus we have ξερός, Ionic for ξηρός, ἀνάθεμα for ἀνάθημα, and in modern Greek, θερίον for θηρίον, βάρεμα for βάρημα, φόρεμα for φόρημα.

In modern Greek, too, it is often difficult to tell whether the η in an unaccented syllable partakes more of the ε or ι sound, for instance, when the word κηρίον is pronounced by a Greek, it is very hard to say whether the η sounds more like ε or ι.

This is, however, partly due to the fact that it is immediately followed by an accented syllable, on which the stress of the voice is laid, so that the η sound is not so clearly distinguished.

From all this collected evidence it would seem that η, in the fourth century B.C., was an intermediate sound between ε and ι, now pronounced just like ι or English *e* in *be*.

υ.

Now pronounced just like ι or English "e" in "be."

In very early times it would seem that υ was pronounced like ου (German u or English oo), but as early as the fifth century B.C. we find ι written instead of υ, from which we may assume that gradually the sound of υ had come to be something between that of ου and ι, perhaps like the German ü or French u. The ι sound appears to have prevailed more and more until at the beginning of the Christian era, if not sooner, there was no perceptible difference between υ and ι. We might conclude, therefore, that the pronunciation of υ passed, as it were, through three stages : oo, ü, ee—we find the same three gradations in German, "funf" in O.H.G., now "fünf," which in South Germany is pronounced "finf."

We find instances of the interchange of υ and ι at an early period even in Attic. This interchange was not general but only occurred in a few words, *e.g.* in βιβλίον (a foreign word) which is also written βυβλίον, and in ἥμισυ which in *C.I.A.* ii., 17, *A.* 45, an inscription of 378 B.C. and on all later ones is written ἥμυσυ ; beyond these words, it occurs in proper names of obscure meaning, thus we have Μουνυχίων and Μουνιχίων, Ἀμφικτύονες and Ἀμφικτίονες.

In some cases υ and ι were interchanged in the same word, such interchange may perhaps be due to assimilation and there may have been variation in pronunciation as well as in writing ; for example, we have writings such as Μιτυλήνη and Μυτιλήνη.

Outside Attica we also have numerous examples of υ for ι
and ι for υ; thus on Laconian inscriptions we find Τινδαρίδαι
for Τινδαρύδαι (v. Röhl. 62, *a*), and Ἐλευΰνια for Ἐλευσίνια
(v. Röhl. 79, 11). On Corinthian vases of an apparently early date (cf. *Dial.
Inschr.* 3135 and 3130), Τσμήνα stands for Ἰσμήνη, and Κιανίς
for Κυανίς.

For this confusion between υ and ι, we may compare the
different forms, " Hülfe " and " Hilfe," " gültig " and " giltig," &c.,
in German, and the fact that in Southern Germany *ü* is
always *i*. So in the Æolic dialect of ancient Greek ι
was written for the Attic υ, *e.g.* ἴψος, ἰψηλός (for ὕψος,
ὑψηλός).

On the other hand, as evidence for υ having at one time
been sounded similarly to ου, we have the fact that in the
Æolic dialect, and especially in Bœotia, ου was often written
for Attic υ, whence the forms θουγάτηρ (Æolic), οὔδωρ, κοῦμα,
κοῦνες from Bœotia.

This old ου sound is still retained in some of the modern
dialects; thus in the Chian dialect we have κιουρά for κυρία,
and in the Laconian νιουττά for νύκτα, and even in all parts
of Greece ου is now written and spoken in many words which
were formerly written with an υ: as examples we may give
μουστάκιον from ancient μύσταξ, σκούτιον from σκύτος.

Its great resemblance to the iota sound is also shown by its
being sometimes interchanged with ει, as in the word Φλειάσιοι
which occurs for Φλυάσιοι in the inscription on the bronze
stand of the gold tripod, which the Greeks dedicated at Delphi
c. 475 B.C. after the battle of Platæa; and on their drachmas
of 430 B.C. we also find Φλειασίων.

In Latin υ was first transcribed by " u " and later, in Cicero's time, by "y", thus we have mus from μῦς, sus from σῦς, cuprum from κύπρον, and onyx from ὄνυξ, herpyllum from ἕρπυλλον, Cyprus for Κύπρος. We cannot conclude much from the former of these transliterations, as we do not know what the exact pronunciation of the Latin u was; but that it was not the exact equivalent for the Greek υ, we learn from Quintilian (xii. 10, 27) who, speaking of the Latin language, says: "Iucundissimas ex Græcis litteras non habemus (υ et φ) quibus nullæ apud eos dulcius spirant."

ω.

In the modern language there is no difference between the sounds of ω and ο, they are both pronounced alike, somewhat as the English o in 'core.'

The Greeks themselves and all Reuchlinians are agreed in thinking, that in the classical period there was more distinction between them; and the most palpable proof of this is that, if ο and ω had been pronounced alike, ω would not have been introduced into the alphabet in 403 B.C.; but whether the distinction was only one of quantity or also one of quality, it is impossible to say.

Its early tendency to become ο, especially in unaccented syllables, seems to be shown by the accentuation of such words as μονόκερως, ῥινόκερως and of the genitives in -εως and -εων, e.g., πόλεως, δυνάμεων.

Outside Greece proper, e.g., in Egypt, the greatest confusion prevailed in the usage of ο and ω as early as the third and second centuries B.C.; thus on papyri of the Ptolemæan period we find such spellings as:—ὠκταετηρίδα, ὡρᾶται, μείζων, μεθοπορινός, &c. This interchange of *o* and *ω* is also found on Greek inscriptions, but not very frequently on those of the best time.

αι

αι is now pronounced like *ε* or English *ey* in 'they.' The Erasmians maintain that it was pronounced as a diphthong till 30 B.C., if not later, because Dionysius of Halicarnassus finds fault with the phrase 'καὶ 'Αθηναίων' in Thucydides because, as he says, "the sounds of the *ι* and *a* do not blend." But what does that mean? If αι be pronounced as a diphthong, why should the *a* of 'Αθηναίων not sound well after the *ι* of the καὶ, which pronounced as a diphthong would be καἰ? There are many words, *e.g.*, "Ιακχος, ἰατρός, in which *a* follows *ι* without producing a disagreeable effect. The objection seems to be meaningless and unworthy of any serious consideration; Dionysius did not even know how Thucydides pronounced the words, and yet he tries to correct him.

Secondly, some grammarians, in order to distinguish αι from ᾳ, call the former ἡ αι δίφθογγος ἡ ἔχουσα τὸ ι ἐκφωνούμενον and this definition does not seem applicable to αι pronounced like *ε*. These grammarians may, however, only have been referring to the fact that in αι the *ι* was sometimes pronounced, *i.e.*, in those cases where we should write it *aï*, whereas in ᾳ it never was pronounced.

Other grammarians, again, distinctly state that αι was not pronounced *aï*. For instance, the illustrious grammarian, Herodian, who lived in the earlier half of the second century, A.D. draws a distinction between words spelt with *ε* and αι, *e.g.*, between πέδαι, κενός and παῖδες, καινός by saying that the former should be *written* διὰ τοῦ ε ψιλοῦ, the latter διὰ τῆς αι διφθόγγου, which proves that in his time the educated Greeks of Alexandria and Rome pronounced ε and αι alike. Sextus Empiricus, too, calls αι a φθόγγος μονοειδής and a στοιχεῖον.

In the language itself the numerous collateral forms of words spelt with either αι or ε, afford strong proof of the early resemblance between the sounds αι and ε; such forms are αἰώρα (Plato), and ἐώρα, (Sophocles), φαίναξ and φέναξ, αἰόλλω and ἑίλω, ἀνώγαιον and ἀνώγεον, and the derivatives, γεώγραφος, γεώμετρος and others from the word γαῖα. This interchange of αι and ε is also found on Attic and other inscriptions; thus on nearly all the Attic inscriptions of the fifth and fourth centuries B.C. we find the form Ποτιδεᾶται *e.g.* (in C. I. A. i. 244) on an inscription of *c*. 436 B.C. (cf. also C. I. A. i. 240, 241, 242), but on the bronze stand of the gold tripod which the Greeks dedicated at Delphi in the year 475 B.C. the form Ποτιδαιᾶται is used.

Further, we find Ἀλκμεωνίδης for Ἀλκμαιωνίδης on two inscriptions, one of 460 B.C., the other of 373 B.C. (v. C. I. A. 433 and *ib.* i. p. 254), and again Ἀλκμεωνίδου on one of the earlier half of the fourth century B.C. (cf. C. I. A. 946).

Αὐλεᾶται occurs for Αὐλαιᾶται on two inscriptions of the fifth century B.C. (cf. C. I. A., i. 229 and 237.) An inscription from Megara of the third century B.C. has κέκρυπτε, δόξες and μυρίες for κέκρυπται, δόξαις and μυρίαις (v. C. I. G., 1051, 1066), Ross (*Inser. gr. ined.* iii. 246) gives an inscription of the first century B.C. on which κῆτε occurs for κεῖται.

In the Septuagint the Hebrew *e* is regularly transcribed by the Greek αι, *e.g.*, Βαιθηλ for Bethel, Αἴλαμ for Elam. On the inscriptions of the Christian era, the examples of this interchange are much more frequent; for instance, we have προθυρέους for προθυραίους on one of 211 A.D. (v. Fröhner, 29) and Ἀηνέωνος for Ἀηναίωνος on another of 201 A.D. (v. Latyshev, *Inscr. gr. orae septent. Pont. Eux.*, No. 3).

Further evidence against the broad pronunciation of αι is given us by Aristophanes, in the following passage from the *Clouds* ll., 870, ff.

PHID.   εἰ κρέμαιό γε.

SOCR. ἰδοῦ κρέμαι', ὡς ἠλίθιον ἐφθέγξατο
         καὶ τοῖσι χείλεσιν διερρυηκόσιν.

Only the Erasmian pronunciation of αι as German *ai* suits this description.

In *Latin* αι was transcribed by *ae, e.g.*, *aether* from αἰθήρ, *aenigma* from αἴνιγμα, *musae* from μοῦσαι, *vae* from Fαι, and as the pronunciation of Latin *ae* is now almost universally admitted to have been like the German *ä* or English 'ay' in 'day,' it would follow from this transcription that the Greek αι was also pronounced like our 'ay' in 'day,' that is like the Greek ε. Plutarch transcribes both Latin *ae* and *e* by αι, for 'fenestra' he writes φαινέστρα, for Caecilius, Καικίλιος, but also Κεκίλια as well as Καικίλια. So too, Dionysius of Halicarnassus (fl. 30 B.C.), writes Πρενεστῖνοι for Praenestini, whereas, Strabo and others write Πραινεστῖνοι: and on inscriptions and coins of the time of the Caesars ε is often put for αι, *e.g.*, on a coin of Nero's of 69 A.D., Ποππέα is written for Ποππαία. These examples show that there was apparently no difference in pronunciation between the Latin *ae* and the Greek αι and ε.

The accentuation of words ending in -αι and the treatment of αι in prosody also argue against the broad pronunciation of it as German *ai*. For, if αι = *ai*, how can the accentuation of words like καίνυμαι, ἐπιστάμεναι, λύσασθαι, ὅμοιαι, δείλαιαι be reconciled with the fact that the Greeks never accented a word on the propenultimate unless the final syllable was short? It is very hard to imagine that a broad sound like the German ai or English ī in " wine" could be accounted short in prosody, yet it must be done if the Erasmian pronunciation is correct, for -αι is constantly scanned as a short syllable when it is a flexional ending and even in καί in Homer. These difficulties at once disappear if the traditional pronunciation of αι as ε be accepted as correct, for then αι can be equivalent to either long or short ε, as the metre or accentuation requires.

The arguments to be drawn from Elision and Crasis may next be considered.

The syllable -αι, when it is a verbal ending, can in most cases suffer elision, and examples of this elision are numerous, not only in Homer, but even in the Attic comedians and prose, e.g. Il. i. 117, βούλομ' ἐγώ. Aristoph. Nub. 780, πρὶν τὴν ἐμὴν καλεῖσθ', ἀπαγξαίμην τρέχων. The αι of the word καί is also elided sometimes, though not very frequently, at least in Attic; as instances of its elision we may give: Soph. Antig. 344, κ'οὐδὲν ἀνθρώπου δεινότερον πέλει, and Aristoph. Nub. 1181, χ'οἷον τὸν υἱὸν ἐκτρέφεις. On the Gortynian inscriptions (5th cent. B.C.) καὶ becomes κ' before a vowel almost without exception, e.g., κ'ἀποστᾶ, κ'ἀνέρ, κ'ε &c.

The Erasmians argue that this elision can be easily explained from the pronunciation of αι as German ai; ai, they say, easily loses its i sound and becomes ă and then this ă is elided:—but how can this assertion be proved? A much more plausible explanation is that αι was, as now, pronounced like ε, and that this simple vowel sound was dropped before a similar or a stronger vowel sound.

The question of Crasis seems a very difficult one to explain, and does not appear to be of much use for ascertaining the pronunciation of the vowels and diphthongs concerned. In Crasis quite a different vowel sound seems often to be produced rather than a combination of the two original sounds; this may be illustrated by such Crases as κᾆτα from καὶ εἶτα, and μοὖστίν from μοι ἐστίν, for, if the separate words be pronounced either according to the Erasmian or the traditional pronunciation, in either case the contracted form contains a vowel sound which is not heard in the separate words. Most probably these Crases were little used in speaking but were stereotyped forms of writing, based on the principle of dropping the middle one of the three vowels, when there were three, and contracting the other two according to the regular rules for contraction. A very good example of a Crasis, in which the two original vowel-sounds are replaced by quite a different one, and which can hardly have been pronounced as it is written, is θἄτερον from τὸ ἔτερον.

εἰ.

εἰ now = ι or English " e " in " be."

The Erasmians pronounce it like German ei or English long ī, but there are no proofs whatever that it was ever so pronounced, and they themselves admit that its pronunciation had become quite assimilated with that of iota, by the second century B.C.

On the other hand we have numerous proofs of its resemblance to ι. A large number of very old words are written with either ει or ι, e.g. εἴω and ἴω, στείβω and στίβω; and in Homer and Hesiod we find the collateral forms εἴκελος and ἴκελος, γείνομαι and γίνομαι, εἶσος and ἶσος, ἐρείκω and ἐρίκω.

In the Bœotian dialect ι is found for ει on very early inscriptions, e.g. ἴκατι (for εἴκοσι), αἰ (for ἀεί).

On the Gortynian inscription (fifth century B.C.) πρεὶν is found for πρίν; and πλῖον, πλίονος, πλίονα for πλεῖον, πλείονος, πλείονα respectively.

On many Elean inscriptions of the classical period ι occurs for ει, e.g. Ἴρις for Εἶρις, φίδιον for φείδιον, τειμᾶς for τιμᾶς. The forms ἐτείμησαν, τειμαῖς are found on nearly all the Carian inscriptions in the C.I.G. pp. 511 ff.

That ει was pronounced like ι in Plato's time can be inferred from the two following etymologies—

(a) Cratyl. 402, E. ὠνόμασε Ποσειδῶνα ὡς ποσίδεσμον ὄντα.

(b)   „   408, B. ἡ γε Ἴρις ἀπὸ τοῦ εἴρειν ἔοικε κεκλημένη.

Again, on Attic inscriptions we only find the forms in ι of Ποσιδεών and Χίρων (cf. C.I.G. 7400, 8359); Χείρων is only once found on an unreliable inscription.

In C.I.A. i. 463 we have οἰκτίρω for οἰκτείρω.

The ending -κλίδης is often found instead of -κλείδης, e.g. (Dial. Inschr. 3121) Χαρικλίδας.

An Athenian inscription of the end of the fifth century B.C. has ἐπίθοντο for ἐπείθοντο (cf. Fröhn. p. 198, 15).

From 200 B.C. there seems to have been very great confusion in the use of ει and ι. Frequently ει was put for ι, e.g. πολείτης, and thus a wrong orthography was propagated, e.g. τίω should be τείω, and probably οἰκτείρω should be οἰκτίρω, and ἱμάτιον, εἱμάτιον. For further examples we may refer to an inscription of the second century B.C. (v. C.I.G. 5594) where the forms ῥινός, ῥῖνα stand side by side with ῥεινός, ῥεῖνα; and to the inscriptions from Stiris of 180 B.C., where the forms Στείριοι, Στιρίων, Στειρίων, Στιρίαν are used without any distinction (v. *Dial. Inschr.* 1539 ff.).

On the papyri, too, of the second century B.C. ει and ι are used indifferently one for the other.

The Septuagint consistently renders the Hebrew *i* by ει, *c.g.* χερουβείμ (= Cherubim).

After the beginning of the Christian era, the examples of ει for ι, and *vice versâ*, can be found on nearly every inscription; as instances we may mention the writings πείονα (for πίονα), τειμήσατε (for τιμήσατε), σίσασα (for σείσασα) which are found on the inscription on the statue to the wife of Herodes Atticus (second century A.D.), and also the following, which are taken from Latyshev's *Inscr. grace. et lat. orae septent. Pont. Eux.*:

αἵμνηστος (for ἀείμνηστος), ἐπιδὴ (for ἐπειδὴ), γεινώσκειν (for γινώσκειν), μειμεῖσθαι (for μιμεῖσθαι), ἰς τὴν ἀκρείβειαν (for εἰς τὴν ἀκρίβειαν), 'Αφροδείτη (for 'Αφροδίτη), ἐξάγιν (for ἐξάγειν). All these date from the first and second centuries A.D.

We have also the grammarians' testimony to prove that ει was by them considered to be one simple sound: cf. Sextus Empiricus who says "ὁ τοῦ ει φθόγγος ἁπλοῦς ἐστι καὶ μονοειδής." And Aulus Gellius, who evidently considered that ει was superfluous and might have been represented by ι, when he wrote the following remark : "Graecos non tantae inscitiae arcesso, qui ου ex ο et υ scripserunt, quantae qui ει ex ε et ι ; illud enim inopia fecerunt, hoc *nulla re subacti.*"

We have thus shown that from the earliest times there is continuous and frequent proof of the interchange of ει and ι. From the end of the third century B.C. it is universally admitted to have been equivalent in sound to iota; the modern pronunciation shows no distinction. We have, accordingly, uninterrupted evidence for its pronunciation as ι (*i.e.* as English "e" in "be") for a period of more than 2000 years.

οι.

Now pronounced like ι, or our English "e" in "be."

This diphthong is one of the oldest in the Greek language and is found on inscriptions long before 403 B.C., when ει and ου were first introduced; therefore it had, at the beginning of the fourth century B.C., been already several centuries in use, and its sound may by that time have already become assimilated to that of iota, even if *originally* the two distinct sounds of o and ι were heard in its pronunciation.

We have not, however, any proofs that it ever was pronounced like *oï* or *oy*, all the evidence we have tends to prove its great similarity to the υ and ι sounds.

Its close relationship to υ and ι is demonstrated by the kindred words κοίρανος and κύριος, λυγρὸς and λοιγός, and the collateral forms φλοία and φλία, γλοία and γλία, and many others which we have in Attic. Very many old words in all the dialects can be correctly written either with οι or υ; such are κοῖλον or κῦλον, δρύτη and δροίτη, οἶδνον and ὕδνον, ψοία or ψύα, ῥοῖκος or ῥύκος. Some dialects, especially the Æolic, often write υ for Attic οι; thus the Boeotians write ἐμὺ, καλὺ, τῦς ἄλλυς, ἔχυ, for Attic ἐμοί, καλοί, τοῖς ἄλλοις, ἔχοι.

The belief that it was pronounced more like υ than any other vowel is strengthened by the fact that the grammarians named it 'υ διὰ διφθόγγου' to distinguish it from ὗψιλον.

The interchange of οι and υ is also found on the papyri of the second century B.C.; thus ἀνύγετε and ἀνύγω on one of

160 B.C. In the first and second centuries A.D. the examples of
this interchange on Greek inscriptions are numerous; thus
λυπά, νεωπνῶν, πεπύημαι, for λοιπά, νεωποιῶν, πεποίημαι, are
found on inscriptions from Aphrodisias (v. *C.I.G.* 2824, 2826);
οἰπὸ (for ὑπὸ) on a Lydian one of the year 126 A.D. (v. *Bull. de
corr. hell.* viii. 378); also ἀνῦξαι and ἀνύξι on one from
Cephallenia (*C.I.G.* 1933).

The most conclusive argument for establishing the similarity
in sound of οι and ι and for refuting the assertion that in the
days of Pericles οι was pronounced *oy* is to be taken
from Thucydides, bk. ii. ch. 54. Here, in speaking of the
pestilence which ravaged Athens during the first years of the
Peloponnesian war, he says that the Athenians began to recall an
old oracle which had foretold a disaster of the kind in the words :

Ἥξει δωριακὸς πόλεμος καὶ λοιμὸς (or λιμὸς) ἅμ᾽ αὐτῷ,

and after quoting the oracle, he goes on to say that the people
questioned whether it was λιμός, a famine, or λοιμός, a pestilence, that had been foretold (ἐγένετο μὲν οὖν ἔρις τοῖς ἀνθρώ-
ποις μὴ λοιμὸν ὠνομάσθαι ἐν τῷ ἔπει ὑπὸ τῶν παλαιῶν, ἀλλὰ
λιμόν . . . .). Now if λοιμός had at that time been pronounced
" loymos " whilst λιμός was pronounced " leemos," the sounds of
the words would have been so very different that there could
not have been any doubt as to which had been said. It proves,
consequently, that ι and οι were either pronounced exactly alike,
or that the difference was so very slight as to be almost
imperceptible to the ear.

From Aristophanes we get further evidence against the
broad pronunciation of οι as *oï*; in the *Pax*, l. 932 one man
jeers at another for exclaiming οἴ and calls it an Ἰωνικὸν ῥῆμα ;
and a few lines further down, ʽ ἵνα λέγωσ᾽ Ἰωνικῶς οἴ.ʼ

That οι was in the third century B.C. pronounced just the same as η and consequently as ι (because η at that time was probably = ι) we can infer from a passage in the Περὶ ἑρμηνείας of Demetrius Phalereus : the words are ἐν τῷ οἵην οὐ μόνον διαφέροντα τὰ γράμματα, ἀλλὰ καὶ οἱ ἦχοι, ὁ μὲν δασὺς, ὁ δὲ ψιλός, ὥστε πολὺ ἀνόμοια εἶναι. From this it is clear, in the first place, that Demetrius speaks of only *two* syllables in οἵην—and thus considers οι a monophthong—and, in the second place, that, when drawing attention to the dissimilarity of the two syllables οι- and -ην, he refers to it as being only one of orthography, not of pronunciation. This conclusion seems perfectly legitimate, because on any other supposition there would have been no necessity for his drawing attention to the fact at all.

Other evidence for its similarity to the *i* sound is derived from its Latin substitute often being *i;* thus the case-ending of the nom. plur. of masc. and fem. nouns of the second declension, is -οι in Greek and *i* in Latin, *e.g.* ἄνεμοι and animi; also the dat. plur.-οις is -*is* in Latin, ἀνέμοις, animis. We further have such words as vinum fr. οἶνος, vicus fr. οἶκος, mihi fr. μοι; also "mira" for μοίρα in Sidonius and "solicismus" in Arsenius.

On the other hand, οι is generally transcribed by *oe*, *e.g.* oeconomus, oenopolus, oestrus, from οἰκονόμος, οἰνοπώλος, οἶστρος, and from this transcription some Erasmians, who think that *oe* was a real diphthong as late as the second century A.D. argue that οι must have been a diphthong as long as *oe* was. However, the pronunciation of *oe* is unknown; it may perhaps have been an intermediate sound between *o* and *e*, something like the Germ. ö ; all we know for certain about it is, that it was constantly interchanged with *u*. Thus we have " plura " and "ploera," " moenia " and " munia," " moenio " and " munio," " Punicus " and

'' Pocnicus," " uti " and " oeti " &c. ; sometimes it is even interchanged with *i*, *e.g.* "locbertas" and "libertas." From this it follows that the transcription *oe* for *οι* does not prove anything about the pronunciation of *οι*.

The Erasmians adduce Crasis also as a means of proving that *οι=oy*. They argue that in a Crasis like μούστίν from μοι ἐστίν *οι* if pronounced like *oy* could easily lose its *i* sound, and then the *o + ε* of ἐστιν would produce the sound *ου ;* but is it not rather a *petitio principii* to take it for granted that *oy* in certain cases becomes *o* ? Is it not more probable that the form μούστὶν tells us nothing about the pronunciation ? in writing the middle one of the three vowels, *ι*, was naturally dropped, and the *o* and *ε* coming together were, as always, written *ου*.

Again, they argue that the Crasis θοιμάτιον from τὸ ἱμάτιον proves that the sound *oy* was pronounced as well as written. Can we not maintain with greater probability that the two vowels were kept in writing, but in speaking the short *o* of that unimportant word, the article, was scarcely, if at all, heard, so that the *ι* alone was distinctly heard and θοιμάτιον was pronounced like θιμάτιον ? On the other hand, if after contraction, the contraction itself was still pronounced *thoymation* in such a way as to let both the *o* and *ι* sounds be distinctly heard, then no real Crasis had taken place, for the pronunciation, and the aspirate of the *ι* would hardly have affected the *τ*.

We may safely say that Crases at the best prove but very little : if *οι = oy* why should ἐγὼ οἶμαι not produce " egoimai " instead of " egomai " (ἐγῶμαι), since the sound *oy* is fuller and stronger than that of *ō* ?

We have still to take into consideration the question as to how *οι* was treated in prosody.

We shall find when so doing that there is no uniform treatment; but that sometimes it is counted as a short syllable, whereas at others, and more frequently, it reckons as a long one.

Now it is true that its treatment in prosody as a long syllable is more frequent than its usage as a short one, but on the other hand if we could conceive a long diphthong of the full sound *oy* to have been accounted short in mètre, we should have to subvert all our notions about long and short syllables. In Homer, however, οι is scanned as a short syllable not only when it is a flexional ending, or an unaccented word, but even when it is the accentuated and principal syllable of a word.

e.g. *Odys.* xiv. 224 : Ἀλλά μοῖ αἰεὶ νῆες ἐπήρετμοι φίλαι ἦσαν.

Odys. vii. 312 : Τοῖος ἐὼν, οἵός ἐσσι, τά τε φρονέων ἅτ᾽ ἐγώ περ.

Il. xiii. 275 : Οἶδ᾽ ἀρετὴν οἵός ἐσσι· τί σε χρὴ ταῦτα λέγεσθαι;

Il. ii. 468 : Μυρίοι, ὅσσα τε φύλλα καὶ ἄνθεα γίγνεται ὥρῃ.

In the Attic tragedians and comedians, οι is also constantly found short in the word τοιοῦτος, and the phrase οἶός τε, and even in ποιεῖν and one or two other words.

e.g. Soph. *Oed. Tyr.* 1428 : Οὐδεὶς οἵός τε πλὴν ἐμοῦ φέρειν βροτῶν.

ib. *Oed. Tyr.* 543 : οἶσθ᾽ ὡς ποίησον ; ἀντὶ τῶν εἰρημένων.

ib. *Oed. Tyr.* 140 : κἄμ᾽ ἂν τοιαύτῃ χειρὶ τιμωρεῖν θέλοι.

Whilst there would be considerable difficulty in treating οι as a short syllable in scansion, if we gave it the broad pronunciation *oy* there is not the same difficulty in making its quantity long if we pronounce it as our " e " in " be," that is like ι, to which its modern pronunciation is equivalent.

υι.

now pronounced like iota, that is like English " e " in " be." υι was a so-called spurious diphthong, and only found before a vowel in the ordinary language, and it very soon was simplified to υ. In Attic there is hardly a trace of it left in the fourth century B.C. On the inscriptions of that century υ is always written for υι, e.g. ὑὸς for υἱὸς, 'Ωρείθυα for · 'Ωρείθυια, κατεαγυᾶ (for -γυῖα), πεπλευκύας (for -κυίας).

On the Attic inscriptions of the fifth century υἱ still occurs, thus we have υἱὸς on the altar of Peisistratos (*C.I.A.* iv. 373 c), and ἐσεληλυθυίας repeatedly in *C.I.A.* i. 273.

In Hellenistic Greek the writing υι before a vowel was brought in again, and was thus reintroduced into the Attic authors. It also reappears occasionally on Attic inscriptions after the second century B.C., and in the time of the emperors it is much more frequent in words where it had originally stood than the simple υ.

That it was a single sound even as early as Homer's time is proved by the fact that υι- always counts as one syllable in his poems (and we may also notice in the word υἱὸς its quantity is generally short).

cf. *Il.* vi. 130: Οὐδε γὰρ, οὐδὲ Δρύαντος υἱὸς, κρατερὸς Λυκούργος.

Il. iv. 473: 'Ενθ' ἔβαλ' 'Ανθεμίωνος υἱὸν Τελαμώνιος Αἴας.

Il. vii. 47: "Εκτορ, υἱὲ Πριάμοιο, Διὶ μῆτιν ἀτάλαντε.

In Attic poetry υἱὸς is always written and scanned as ὑὸς. The υ and ι seem to have been contracted into long υ. The υ is also long on metrical inscriptions, as in *C.I.A.* iv. 373, 218. υι is also interchanged with ει. Thus on the Heraclean tables we have ἐρρηγείας seven times for ἐρρηγυίας; and also γεγονεῖα for γεγονυῖα on an Attic inscription of the second century B.C. (v. *C.I.A.* ii. 455, 16).

From all evidence, therefore, υι was equivalent to υ in the Attic language of the fourth century, and hence its sound was very nearly, if not quite, the same as that of ι.

αυ, ευ.

These are now pronounced like English *af*, *ef*, except when they come before a vowel, a liquid or a medial and then they are pronounced like *av*, *ev*, respectively.

The Erasmians pronounce them like German *au* and *eu* respectively, for they maintain that in these diphthongs the υ must have had its original *u* sound (like English *oo* in "boot") and cannot have been = German *ü* or French *u*, as the modern pronunciation could not have developed itself from *aü*, *eü*, whereas it could have done so from *au*, *eu*. This explanation is very unsatisfactory, difficult to understand and only based on a hypothesis; but, on the other hand, we have definite proofs that αυ and ευ early tended to become *av* and *ev*, as they are now.

The most important proof is, that there are many examples of ϝ being written instead of υ after a and ε. The greatest number of these are to be found on the Cretan inscriptions where ϝ is constantly written instead of υ or placed before or after it; *e.g.* ὠϝτό (= αὐτό); ἀϝτός; ἀϝυτάν; ἐϝεργεσίας;

'ΑϜλῶνι (= Αὐλῶνι); τιτωνϜέσθω (v. Comparetti, *Mus. Ital.*
ii. p. 131, pp. 162 ff.).

Again, on the Cyprian inscriptions Ϝ is regularly placed after
υ, as in ΕὐϜέλθοντος, ΕὐϜαγόρω, κατεσκεύϜασε and other words
(cf. Deecke, *Cypr. Inschr.*).

We have also several valuable single instances of this interchange of υ and Ϝ: thus on a Locrian inscription (cf. Röhl. 321,
B. 15), there is one instance of ΝαϜπακτίων among about
twenty of Ναυπακτίων.

᾿ΕϜθετος (for εὔθετος) is found on a Corinthian tablet.
ΤεϜυκρος for Τεῦκρος occurs on a Lacedæmonian inscription
(v. Rang. *Antiq. hell.* ii. 1). Kirchhoff (*Stud.* p. 86) mentions
an old Naxian inscription which has ἀϜυτο (for αὐτό), and a
Corcyrean one of the seventh or sixth century B.C., on which
ἀϜυτάν and ἀριστεύϜοντα occur. Again, on an Elean inscription
(*C.I.G.* No. 11) which Boeckh assigns to the period between
Ol. 40 and Ol. 60, the name ΕὐϜαίοις occurs, for which he
proposes reading 'ΗρϜαίοις, as he thinks the village Εὔα in the
Peloponnese too insignificant to be the subject of this inscription,
and also that the Υ which is rather squashed in at the end of
a line may be a badly written Ρ. The latter reason, however,
is hardly supported by facts, as the letter is quite distinct and
evidently meant to be a Υ.

We further have examples of the substitution of β for υ.
A Corcyrean inscription (cf. *C.I.G.* 1563) has εὐδομήκοντα (for
ἑβδομήκοντα), and a Boeotian one εὔδομος for ἕβδομος. On
some of the papyri ῥαῦδος and ῥαῦτος are found for ῥάβδος.
A later inscription of uncertain date B.C. gives us the form
κατεσκέβασε (= κατεσκεύασε).

This interchange of β and υ cannot be compared with the
vocalisation of λ into υ (*e.g.* αὐκή for ἀλκή), which is not only

found in Greek but also plays an important part in all the Romance languages.

Turning from substitution and interchange in the language itself to transcription in a foreign tongue, we find that the Latin *av* and *cv* were at first transcribed into Greek by *αου* and *ευ*, *e.g.* Ὀκτάουιος, Σεουῆρος, but from the time of Hadrian onwards they are rendered by *αυ* and *ευ*, *e.g.* Ὀκτάυιος and Σευῆρος. It is certain, therefore, that from the second century A.D. *αυ* and *ευ* were = *av* and *cv*.

On an inscription from Dodona (v. Karapanos, xxxiv. 3) the name Evandros is transcribed sometimes by Εὔανδρος, at others by Εὔβανδρος.

Again, Ulfilas regularly transcribes *αυ*, *ευ* by *av*, *cv*. Thus we have trustworthy evidence that, for at least sixteen or seventeen centuries *αυ* and *ευ* have been pronounced as they are pronounced to-day, whereas we have none at all to support the assumption that they were ever pronounced like German *au* and *cu* (*i.e.* English *ow* and *oy*).

We have still to consider the questions of accent and prosody. As regards the accent, the argument brought against the pronunciation of these diphthongs as *av* and *cv*, is that if they had been so pronounced when accents were introduced, they would never have been marked with a circumflex. To this may be answered that *αυ*, *ευ* are only signs, and by force of analogy they were accented in the same manner as *ου* or any other diphthong.

The question connected with prosody is a less simple one, but here also it does not seem a matter of very great difficulty to account satisfactorily for their quantity, on the assumption that their pronunciation was as that of English *av*, *ev*, or Greek *αβ*, *εβ*. The Erasmians argue that if pronounced as *αβ*, *εβ* (av, ev) their quantity in prosody should always be short. But is this necessarily so? What is there to prevent us from saying that αυ, ευ may = ᾱβ, ε̄β or ᾰβ, ε̆β, as an a and ε may always be pronounced either long or short, and then the one vowel being long would account for their usual quantity in prosody.

Another consideration to be borne in mind is that αυ and ευ are not always long, but are also scanned as short syllables, not only in Homer, but even occasionally in authors of the classical period.

e.g. Hom. *Il.* 20, 334 : Ὃς σευ ἅμα κρείσσων, καὶ φίλτερος ἀθανάτοισι.

Hom. *Il.* xxiv. 595 : Σοὶ δ᾽ αὖ ἐγὼ καὶ τῶνδ᾽ ἀποδάσσομαι, ὅσσ᾽ ἐπέοικεν.

Also in Pindar, *Pyth.* ii. 52 : πολυγαθέες ἀλλά νιν ὕβρις εἰς ἀυάταν ὑπεράφανον.

Soph. *Oed. Col.* 143 : Ζεῦ ἀλεξῆτορ.

And in Pindar, *Pyth.* viii. 48 : παλαισμάτεσσι γὰρ ἰχνεύων ματραδελφέους.

Where some read ἰχνέων or οἰχνέων *metri gratiâ*, but such an alteration is not necessary, if ευ be pronounced *ev.* In Alcman we also find ἀείρομέναι.

And it is to be noticed that in the scansion of such lines it is practically impossible to make the syllable sound short if αυ, and ευ are pronounced as English *ow* and *oy.*

To those who deny that such an explanation is convincing we can at least reply that it seems less strange that αυ, ευ, pronounced *av, ev*, should be generally long in metre than that οι, αι pronounced like English *oy* and *ī* should very frequently be short.

Finally, the υ of αυ and ευ is frequently dropped before a consonant, and this can only be satisfactorily accounted for on the assumption that αυ and ευ were, as they are now, pronounced like *af*, *cf*, or *av*, *cv*. Whoever has heard Greek spoken by Greeks, will have noticed that they only pronounce the υ sound of αυ and ευ very slightly before a consonant, in fact it can scarcely be heard and thus is often omitted in writing. With the ancient forms ἀτάρ for αὐτάρ in Homer, ἀτοῦ, ἑατοῦ (for ἀυτοῦ, ἑαυτοῦ), which are frequently found after the first century B.C., we can compare the modern ones γέμα for γεῦμα, ἔμορφος for εὔμορφος, ῥέμα for ῥεῦμα, &c.

Again, the substitution of ω for αυ which is sometimes found in ancient Doric, *e.g.* καππώτας from καταπαύω, may be paralleled by the following forms from the modern popular language : ὤμορφος and ὄμορφος for εὔμορφος.

β.

β now = Engl. *v* in "ever," or Germ. *w* in "ewig"; in other words, β in the Greek of the present day is a spirant.

The Erasmians contend that in ancient Greek this consonant was a *mute*, and they adduce four definite arguments against the possibility of its having been a spirant. These objections are as follows: firstly, Plato calls β a mute (cf. Theætetus, 403, B.); secondly, the Latin *v* is not transcribed by β until the second century A.D., but by ου; thirdly, the βῆ, βῆ, representing the sheep's cry in the line from Cratinus, cannot be read *vee*, *vee*, but the β must be hard ; and fourthly, the Greek β is transcribed by the Latin *b*.

Dealing with each objection separately, we shall first take the statement that " Plato calls β a mute." This is true, but it remains to be shown whether his statement is strictly accurate, and whether he was taking into account its pronunciation in all parts of Greece. Now it can be easily proved that his statement is not absolutely true, as we find that in several parts of Greece β was very early used as a spirant, for in certain dialects it replaces the ϝ, and in others the " spiritus asper." Thus in the Laconian dialect β is used for the ϝ, e.g. βισχύν, βεκάς, also in the Elean, e.g. βοικία ; whilst the Æolians and Dorians used it as the simple aspirate before ρ, e.g. βρόδων (Sappho) for ῥόδων, βράκος for ῥάκος, βίππος for ἵππος ; also before vowels βέδος for ἔδος, βάγνυμι for ἄγνυμι. In the Macedonian dialect it is used for φ, e.g. Βίλιππος, Βρίγες, Βερενίκη for Φίλιππος, Φρύγες, Φερενίκη.

We next come to the assertion that the Latin v is not transcribed by β until the second century A.D. This is incorrect, as we have instances of its being so transcribed as early as the second century B.C.

On a Delphian inscription of 180 B.C. the names Λιβίου, Βιβίου are found for the Lat. Livius, Vivius.

Again, Polybius (fl. 165 B.C.), Dionysius of Halicarnassus (fl. 30 B.C.), and other writers of the two last centuries B.C., render Latin v by β, e.g. Βάρρων for Varro, Αβεντῖνον or Αουεντῖνον for Aventinum. Plutarch almost always writes β for the Lat. v, e.g. Ραβέννα for Ravenna, βῆλον for velum, βήλαυρον for velabrum, Σέρβιος for Servius, &c.

The argument founded on the βῆ, βῆ, of Cratinus is at the best very unreliable, as are all conclusions drawn from the cries of animals as interpreted by written characters—witness the different representations of the cries of the same animal in

different countries. Besides this, the distinction between the
sound of the labial *b* and the spirant *v* is so small as to be of
no practical account in these instances of onomatopeia, which
are in any case only approximate renderings of the original
sound.

Lastly, we have to consider the argument, that β is transcribed by the Latin *b*. To this we may reply, that even if
β and *b* did not exactly correspond in sound, they held the
same place in the two alphabets, and were naturally looked
upon as equivalents, one for the other. And again, we cannot
be sure how the Lat. *b* was pronounced, but we have evidence
to show that if not actually = *v*, it was at least so soft as to
be interchangeable with it; *e.g.* on ancient inscriptions we find
serbus (= servus), bixit (= vixit), venemeritus (= benemeritus),
amavile (= amabile), and on a document dating from the reign
of Numa "Jobis" occurs for "Jovis."

This tendency of Latin *b* to become *v* is also shown by the
fact that in the Romance languages it often has become *v*,
e.g. Lat. *habere*, Fr. *avoir*, Ital. *avere*.

Another fact, which seems to indicate that β at a very early
period was similar in sound to *v*, is that many words, which are
common to both Greek and Latin, are written in Greek with
a β, in Latin with a *v*, *e.g.* βαίνω and venio, βίος and vivo,
βρώσκω and vorax, βιάω and violo, βούλομαι and volo, and
many others.

γ.

γ is now pronounced like the German "*g*" in "Tage"—
a sound between *g* and *h*; before ε and ι it is like Germ. *j* or
Engl. *y*.

Most Erasmians now admit that it became a spirant at a very early period; this is proved by its being frequently omitted when it comes between two vowels and also wrongly inserted to avoid a hiatus. We have numerous instances of this on the papyri, *e.g.* ὑγιγαίνις and ὑιαίνις for ὑγιαίνεις; κλαίγω for κλαίω; ὁλίος for ὀλίγος, &c. In the Bœotian ἰὼν stands for ἐγώ.

The form ἀγήγοχα is sometimes found for ἀγήοχα; thus it occurs twice on an Ægean inscription (v. *C. I. G.* 2139).

For this same omission of γ between two vowels we may compare the modern forms λέω for λέγω, φάω for φάγω, &c.

The jokes of the comedians at the time of the Peloponnesian war against Hyperbolos for his pronunciation of ὀλίγος as ὀλίος also show that γ was already a spirant at that time. Again, the Doric use of γ to replace an initial ϝ clearly demonstrates that it was by nature a spirant, *e.g.* in Doric we find γοῖνος = οἶνος, γᾶδος = ἦδος, γέαρ = ἔαρ, γέτορ = ἔτος, &c.

δ.

δ is now pronounced like English *th* in *then.*

It evidently was a spirant in very early times in some dialects, as on some Elean inscriptions of the sixth century B.C., we find ζ and δ interchanged, *e.g.* ζέ, ζίκαια, 'Ολυμπιάζων, Ζί for δέ, δίκαια, 'Ολυμπιάδων, Διί.

Similarly, in Ionic and Doric ζ and δ are often interchanged; thus Δεύς is Doric for Ζεύς: ἀρίζηλος and ζορκάς are Ionic for ἀρίδηλος and δορκάς, cf. modern Greek μαζί for ὁμαδεῖ. In Doric, again, σδ is written for the Attic ζ, which shows that δ must have been pronounced soft, *e.g.* μουσίσδω = Attic μουσίζω, μελίσδεται = Attic μελίζεται.

Plato's statement (v. *Cratylus* 418, c.) "*νῦν δὲ ἀντὶ τοῦ δέλτα ζῆτα μεταστρέφουσιν*" compels us to believe that δ was pronounced like the spirant *th* even in Attica, as it would hardly have been interchanged with ζ, if it had been pronounced hard like our English *d.*

Another conclusive proof of the soft pronunciation of δ is derived from the fact that it is often inserted to give a softer or fuller sound to a word, *ἀνέρος* becomes *ἀνδρός*; adverbs, as *μίγδα* from *μίγα, κρύβδα* from *κρύφα.*

Contracted forms like *ῥᾶον, ῥᾶστος* for *ῥάδιον, ῥάδιστος* can also only be explained by assuming δ to have been pronounced as a spirant.

The name "mediæ," which was given to the letters β, γ, δ, by the grammarians, also seems to show that they were neither hard mutes, nor real aspirates, but that they partook of the nature of both, in other words, that they were spirants.

ζ.

This letter is pronounced quite soft by the Greeks, like the English *z* in zebra.

There has been much controversy about the nature and quality of it, as some maintained that it was a double letter composed of the two consonant-sounds *ts* or *ds*, others that it was formed from *sd*, and others, again, that it had always been a single letter pronounced as it is to-day.

The first notion is now exploded, for the second there is something to be said, but the third seems to be the correct one. That it had just the same soft sound in the ancient language as it has in the modern, seems to be sufficiently proved by the one fact that ζ is often written for σ before μ and γ, thus in old

Attic ζμικρός, ζμερδάλεος, ζμῆγμα, ζμινύη were written for σμικρός, σμερδάλεος, σμῆγμα, σμινύη (according to Æl. Dion.). Sextus Empiricus (i. 169) says that Σμύρνα and Ζμύρνα, σμίλιον and ζμίλιον were pronounced exactly alike.

On inscriptions, too, ζ is frequently found for σ before μ and γ from the time of Alexander; e.g. on an Argive inscription of that period, Πελαζγικόν occurs for Πελασγικόν (v. Le Bas, ii. 122). In the Ionian dialect δ is changed into ζ while in Bœotic ζ is changed into δ, e.g. Δεύς, μάδδα for Ζεύς, μάζα : both these interchanges are evidence that ζ was a single soft letter.

On the other hand, there are several arguments for its having been a double letter, at least in some dialects.

One is that in Doric and Æolic σδ is written for ζ, e.g. Σδεύς, μουσίσδω, ψιθυρίσδω for Ζεύς, μουσίζω, ψιθυρίζω ; and on Bœotian and Thessalian inscriptions the same words are spelt indifferently with σδ or ζ, e.g. Θεόσδοτος and Θεοζότα.

Even in Attic we have instances where ζ seems to be composed of σδ, as in βύζην = βύσδην, and 'Αθήναζε, θύραζε = 'Αθήνασ-δε, θύρασ-δε, but this may perhaps be explained by saying that the Attic substituted the easier single sound ζ for the more difficult double consonant-sound σδ, as ζ (= z) is very similar in sound to σδ (= sth) only easier to pronounce.

Again, the grammarians Dionysius of Halicarnassus, Dionysius Thrax, Sextus Empiricus, and others say it is composed of σ and δ. (cf. Sext. Emp. p. 622 : διότι τὸ ζ ἐκ τοῦ σ καὶ δ δοκεῖ συγκεῖσθαι.)

The chief argument, however, for ζ being a double letter rests on the fact that in metre it causes the lengthening of the preceding vowel; the only exceptions to this rule are the two names Ζέλεια and Ζάκυνθος, which occur in Homer, and could

E

not be brought into the hexameter verse, if the final vowel of the preceding word were to be lengthened.

e.g. Il. ii. 824 :

Οἱ δὲ Ζέλειαν ἔναιον ὑπαὶ πόδα νείατον Ἴδης.

And there is one line in the *Anthology* where this rule is transgressed,

βαπτίζεται δ᾽ ὕπνῳ γείτονι τοῦ θανάτου.

θ.

θ is pronounced like English "th" in "thin" both by the Greeks themselves and in England, but in Germany it is pronounced like τ, or "t," though there is apparently no foundation for so pronouncing it.

Its character as aspirate is sufficiently attested by the circumstance that the Æolians substituted another aspirate, φ, for it, as φήρα, φλάω, φλίβω for θήρ, θάω, θλίβω.

Again, unless θ were pronounced as an aspirate, there would be no sense in the ridicule Aristophanes bestows upon a Scythian in the *Thesmophoriazousae* for saying κάτησον, τυγάτριον, κατεύδει, instead of κάθησον, θυγάτριον, καθεύδει (v. ll. 1183 ff.).

π AND τ.

π after μ is pronounced by the Greeks like the English "b," and τ after ν like the English "d": similarly, β after μ, and δ after ν are pronounced hard.

The Erasmians say that such a pronunciation of μπ and ντ cannot possibly have existed in ancient Greek, as it would then have been impossible to draw a distinction between words like ἐντός and ἔνδον, ἀνάφαντον and ἀναφανδόν. The simple answer to this objection is, that they were easily distinguished by their accent. The Greeks pronounce, and, it is to be presumed, always have pronounced, the accented syllable of a word very strongly, whilst the unaccented ones are comparatively little heard, hence there would be no difficulty in distinguishing words that were similarly pronounced but differently accented.

In support of the argument that the same modification of sound took place in the ancient language, we may compare the words ἐντελεχέια and ἐνδελεχής in Aristotle, and the double forms Ἀμπρακία and Ἀμβρακία, ἀμπλακεῖν and ἀμβλακεῖν. The name "Stamboul" also, which is a corruption of " εἰς τὴν πόλιν," or rather ἐις τὴμ πόλιν, is another illustration of π after μ, having been pronounced as " b."

σ.

σ has the same sound as our hard hissing " s," and it is only in Germany that it is still pronounced as a soft "s"; Blass, however, admits that there is no reason for not accepting the traditional pronunciation.

It must be pronounced soft before a liquid or a medial, and that this was the same in the ancient language is shown by ζ often being written for it before β, μ, γ, or δ, e.g., Ζμύρνα and Σμύρνα, ζβέννυμι and σβέννυμι.

That it was always pronounced hard is confirmed by the fact that on old Attic and other inscriptions σσ is sometimes found for σ, and, vice versâ, σ for σσ ; thus we have ἄρισστα = ἄριστα (C.I.A. i. 920); πάσσης for πάσης on an Olympian inscription; Λέσσβον = Λέσβον (C.I.A. ii. 52, c); and πράσων for πράσσων on an Opuntian inscription of uncertain date B.C.

E 2

The Aspirate.

The chief dispute with reference to the rough breathing turns on the fact that its pronunciation is now entirely neglected; and this is used as an additional proof that the present pronunciation of Greek differs essentially from that of the classical period. There are, however, several points to be considered relative to its usage in antiquity, which must considerably modify any conclusions that may have been formed as to the distinction between its ancient and modern pronunciation.

In the first place, we have several facts which serve to show that it was probably not sounded even in the fifth and fourth centuries B.C., or that, if sounded at all, its pronunciation was very fluctuating and slight. The most convincing proof of this is the fact that when in 403 B.C. H, which till then had served as the sign of the rough breathing, was introduced into the Attic alphabet as a long vowel, no new sign was added to mark the rough breathing. The signs ⊢ and ⊣ (which afterwards became ' and ') were first used, as it seems, by Aristophanes of Byzantium who lived c. 200 B.C.

Attic inscriptions, again, of the fifth century B.C. often omit H, thus on the one in *C.I.A.* iv. 53, *a*, it is only retained in the word ἱερόν and omitted in all other words where it should have been written.

So, too, the long inscription (v. *C.I.A.* 324) which contains the accounts for the building of the Erechtheion and dates from the year 404 B.C., shows us more than one hundred cases where the H (spiritus asper) is inserted in the wrong place, *e.g.* ἐπὶ, οἰκοῦν, ἐν, Εὔδοξος, ἐργασαμένῳ close to ἐργασαμένῳ, &c., &c.

Blass says that this inscription is evidently the work of a foreigner—but there seems to be no sufficient ground for this assertion.

On the Heraclean tables the two writings ἴσος and ἴσος occur. From this evidence it is clear, not indeed that the rough breathing was never sounded, but that it was certainly not invariably sounded in the fifth and fourth centuries B.C. Secondly, we must bear in mind that neither the Ionic nor the Æolic dialect had the rough breathing, nor is it found in the Gortynian and Cyprian inscriptions.

The weakness of the rough breathing is further demonstrated by the existence of kindred words like ἡμέρα and ἦμαρ; ἠὼς and ἕως; οἶος and εἷς, and by derivatives like Γλαύκιππος from ἵππος.

With reference to the aspiration of the tenues in Attic, Blass is of opinion that this proves that the breathing must still have been sounded, though perhaps very weakly. This, however, does not necessarily follow, as in modern Greek the rough breathing still causes the preceding tenuis to be changed into its corresponding aspirate, although this breathing has, as even the Erasmians admit, been mute for nearly 2000 years; the Greeks of the present day always say ἀφ' ἡμῶν, καθ' ἡμέραν, καθόλου, ἐφημερίς, although they never sound the rough breathing.

In some dialects it may have been sounded up to a later date, as it is regularly represented in Latin by h; but even in Latin the h was often misplaced from the first century B.C.

Finally, the grammarians, who write about the ἦχος δασύς, nearly all lived at a time when it is almost certain that the rough breathing was no longer sounded.

A passage from Demetrius Phalereus (fl. 325 B.C.) has sometimes been adduced to prove that the rough breathing was still
sounded in his time, but on careful examination it seems rather
to prove just the contrary; the passage is the following:
Ἐν τῷ οἵην οὐ μόνον δ ι α φ έ ρ ο ν τ α τὰ γράμματά ἐστιν, ἀλλὰ
καὶ ο ἱ ἦ χ ο ι, ὁ μ ὲ ν δ α σ ὺ ς, ὁ δὲ ψιλὸς, ὥστε πολὺ ἀνόμοια
εἶναι. This, the Erasmians say, proves that the rough breathing was still sounded. But, on the contrary, if it had still been
sounded, why should he call attention to the fact, that the one
syllable of the word had a rough breathing and the other a
smooth one? He is evidently speaking of the orthography, not
of the pronunciation, and wishes to draw attention to the
fact that *in writing* the first syllable should have the rough
breathing.

After having reviewed the various letters singly, it may be
interesting to note a few peculiarities which have persisted in
the language since very ancient times, and which help to prove
that even in details it has changed very little since the classical
period. In the present form of the language we find the same
interchanges of letters and the same modifications of sounds as
in the ancient language. Thus the ancient Doric and Æolic
wrote γ for β, *e.g.* γλέπαρον or γλέφαρον for βλέφαρον : parallel
to this is the modern form γλέπω for βλέπω. The interchange
of λ and ρ is also a feature common both to the ancient and the
present language; from the ancient we may adduce the kindred
words, παῦρος or φαῦρος and φαῦλος ; ἀμέλγω and ἀμέργω,
and from the modern, the popular forms ἀδερφός for ἀδελφός,
ἦρθα for ἦλθον.

As an instance of continuity in modification of sounds we find
that in modern Greek, the final ν of the article, or of any other
short unimportant word, is changed into μ, if the following word

commences with an μ or π, and we have numerous proofs from
inscriptions that this same change took place in classical times.
Thus on an Attic inscription of c. 419 B.C. (cf. *C.I.G.* 76) we find
ἐάμ που, ὅταμ περ, ἐμ πόλει and many similar examples,—
on others, τῶμ μισθώσεων and ὅταμ πέμπῃ (cf. *C.I.G.* 82 and
87), and on the Gortynian inscription, fifth century B.C., τῶμ
πολιατᾶν.

We have endeavoured to show, within narrow limits, that the
present pronunciation used by the Greeks is no novelty, and is
improperly called "modern," since tradition and philological
research show that in most particulars it reaches far back into
the most flourishing times of Hellas, and is even traceable in
the Epics of Homer. There has been an unbroken tradition
for nearly two thousand years in favour of the present pronunciation, and this we have endeavoured to show rests upon
no mere hypotheses. Tradition itself, as seen in the living
language of to-day, is a fact that pleads powerfully for the
heirloom that has been handed down to the Greek nation from
its ancestors, for perhaps nothing clings more tenaciously to a
nation than the pronunciation of its language.

The Erasmians themselves admit, that the present pronunciation is much the same as that which was in use at the
commencement of the Christian era; and with regard to the
continuity of the Greek language we may quote Professor Jebb,
Modern Greece, p. 54: " Old and new Greece are bound together
by language. Latin passing into Romance languages was more
or less disintegrated. Greek was for centuries rude and un-
grammatical, but it was always itself, and itself alone. . . . In
the organic matters of structure and syntax Greek has never
made a compromise with any other language. . . . During the

last eighty years the Greek language has been returning more
and more to the old classical type. . . . The chief difference
now remaining between old and modern Greek is one which
exists between old and modern languages generally—the old is
synthetic, the modern analytic. Thus it has been the unique
destiny of the Greek language to have had, from prehistoric
times down to our own, an unbroken life. Not one link is
wanting in this chain which binds the new Greece to the old."
The opinion of so distinguished a scholar both in ancient and
modern Greek is most weighty.

Similar testimony is borne by Mr. E. A. Freeman, *Fortnightly
Review*, February 1st, 1879 : " There is something more in the
Greek tongue, something more abiding, something which more
nearly touches the general history of mankind, than is to be
found in that view of it which looks on it as dead, ancient,
classical, cut off from modern interests of every kind. I claim
for the Greek its place on the exactly opposite ground, because
it is not dead but living—because, if it is ancient, it is mediæval
and modern no less."

Well could Professor A. P. Pharmacopoulos, teacher of Modern
Greek in the University of Naples, boast in his inaugural lecture
delivered December 18th, 1885 : " La nostra lingua non è la
figlia della lingua antica, ma la lingua antica stessa sotto una
differente forma, non nelle parole, nei verbi e nelle loro de-
clinazioni, ma nello stile, anzi oggidi usiamo frasi che si
incontrano negli scrittori antichi più classici. La lingua
moderna non è che l'antica stessa."

We, however, for a long time have been applying to Greek
the rules of pronunciation of another language, namely the
Latin, and the vocalization of our own tongue, until we have
lost all analogy with the sound and rhythm of the Greek

language as it was and is spoken. We have tried to mummify
Greek whilst it is still alive, tying it up with the bandages of
a dead language, so that in our hands it has almost ceased to
breathe, and can only express itself in such painful sounds as
were never heard, and cannot by any means be understood, in
its native country. It is not surprising that Greeks should be
astonished at such conduct, and that they cannot understand
any one having the courage so to maltreat a language, as to
render it perfectly unrecognizable to the inhabitants of the
country where it has always been spoken, by our "barbarous
habit of murdering the classical tongue by Latin accentuation
and English vocalization," as Professor Blackie says. And all
this is done for a theory, or a mere opinion, repeated from
mouth to mouth often without much thought, or with none at
all, "That the ancient Greeks could not have pronounced as
the moderns do." We may ask why not ? The answer to this
question has never been conclusive, because, resting simply on
hypotheses and assertions, it never can be satisfactory; indeed,
it is becoming less and less so every day, in proportion as
modern Greece and its literature and language are becoming
better known in Western Europe.

The question of teaching Greek with the traditional pronunciation is now being seriously taken up by the Philhellenic
Society of Amsterdam, and by several professors in Germany,
France, and Italy, all of whom maintain, that by teaching the
language in the same way as we teach other modern languages,
we shall obtain much better results in shorter time than by the
present system of teaching Greek.

To those who take an interest in the maintenance of the
study of the classical language, the question of Greek pronunciation and the method of teaching the language is most

important, since the opponents of the study of Greek in our
schools and universities are daily on the increase, and the
number of students becoming less. Most students of mathe-
matics and of natural science, professors and pupils alike, would
banish Greek from the necessary curriculum of studies at our
universities, and have already to some extent succeeded. We
have already got so far that French or German may in some
examinations be substituted for Greek, and in a short time, if
we continue the present system of teaching the language,
Greek will become an optional subject, except perhaps in the
case of theological students. No wonder that the opposition
exists, and that many argue that the study of Greek entails
eight or nine years of useless labour, which in this country is
almost true. But the opposition can hardly be said to be
against the Greek language itself—which most of the opponents
do not, or only indifferently, understand—but against the waste
of time and the poor results of so many years of often disagreeable labour—a labour of Sisyphus, as Constantine Reyer
of Trieste calls it—both for professors and pupils. We think
the only way to preserve the study of Greek is to render its
acquisition more agreeable and rapid, and the results more
satisfactory, by introducing a radical change in the method of
teaching it.

To bring about a thorough reform, it must be learned and
taught as a living tongue, and as much as possible spoken, and
be studied in its entirety, beginning with the modern language,
in which there is sufficient well-written literature, increasing
daily, in the works of S. Tricoupis, Rangabé, Bikelos, Lambros,
Vlachos, and many others. When the student has fairly
mastered the modern style, which he would do as easily as
he does French or German, he should go backward, as it were,

to the ancient authors, thus becoming gradually acquainted
with the more archaic grammatical constructions and forms
of expression, which will present little or no difficulty, but, on
the contrary, prove an interesting study. This method of
studying is the most useful and agreeable way of learning the
language, and enables the student to understand and appreciate
the classical writers a thousandfold better than by the present
system.

This is the true way of learning the ancient literature of any
living tongue; we do not begin to teach or to study French
with the *Chanson de Roland*, nor German with *Gudrun*. We
know that many will be ready to say, that though this way
may apply very well to other languages, yet it does not to
Greek, and the innovation may seem too great or too bold.
We, however, think that it would apply better to Greek than
to most other languages of Europe that we know of, because
there is very much less difference between the Greek of to-day
and that of classical times, than between mediæval French,
German, and English, and these languages as they are spoken
and written at the present time. The *Roman de la Rose*,
Gudrun, *Nibelungenlied*, and *Chaucer* differ much more from
the languages of which they are the early representatives, than
Homer does from the language now spoken and written in
Athens. Of Greek we may truly say: "La lingua moderna
non è che l'antica stessa." The grammar, accidence, and
syntax, remains practically the same as in classical times.

Indeed, the grammars used in the Gymnasia of Greece are
similar to those used in the Gymnasia of Germany and the
public schools of England. Many of them are simply transla-
tions from the German. Therefore to study Greek as a living
language would require no change of grammar; the slight

differences in the future and infinitive of the verbs could easily be explained *vivâ voce*, as they present no difficulty. The principal difference is in the style of the written language, which is simpler than the classical, to which it thus forms an easy introduction. But even with regard to style, we should consider that the classical works which have survived the wreck of ages, do not give us the more popular written and spoken language of their times. It is to be remembered that already in the fourth century B.C., but especially in the Alexandrian period, many provincial peculiarities were being introduced into the Attic dialect, and from this combination arose in the third century B.C. the common dialect, ἡ κοινὴ διάλεκτος, in which different degrees of development are to be noticed, according to the time in which the writers lived, as in the writings of Polybius, Diodorus, Pausanias, and Dio Cassius. The present language is nothing else than a somewhat modernized form of the κοινὴ διάλεκτος of antiquity, and it is with this that we propose the study of Greek should begin. We venture to think that this method would render the study of the language much easier, and make it much more interesting to the pupil, who would thus cease to look with awe upon a language which has hitherto been considered dead and fraught with difficulties. Life and interest would be given to the study, more especially if the language were not only read but spoken. Nearly all the words, at least the roots and simple words, with many expressions of the present spoken and written language, would be constantly met with in the after-study of the classical authors, thus removing difficulties and giving a zest to the study.

By this system the difficulty with regard to accentuation would be almost entirely removed, because, from the very commencement, the pupil would be taught to accentuate the words aright by reading aloud with the proper pronunciation, which necessarily includes accentuation, and by which words of similar orthography, but differing in meaning according to the accentuation, which occur in Greek as in English, are readily distinguished, *e.g.* ἄγων, leading; ἀγών, a contest. A wrong accent in pronunciation would soon be as easily distinguished in Greek as in English, and if the student had any doubt he would only have to pronounce the word aloud to remove the difficulty.

At present the great majority of English students of Greek are quite at a loss about the accentuation. They learn the rules, but the practice remains most difficult, and to the majority an unsolved enigma to the end. No wonder that this should be so, for the majority of words are differently accentuated in the English pronunciation from what they are in the Greek. A curious example of this is found in an edition of some of the Greek tragedies, some years ago, by T. W. C. Edwards, in which he gives an *ordo* of the words with the English accentuation, that the pupil should read the text properly! What should we think of some German author being treated in this way to suit some English theory of pronouncing that language? If it would be absurd to do this with German, why should we do so with Greek? It is true we do not accent Greek words in writing according to the English pronunciation, but we make it even more difficult for our students, for we insist upon their accentuating their written Greek as the Greeks do, and on their reading it with another, and often totally different accentuation. If it were not a fact, we could scarcely believe such a thing credible.

The difficulty of introducing the study of Greek as a living language with the proper pronunciation would not be great as regards the pupils, for they would learn to pronounce Greek more easily than they do French, but it would be with the majority of teachers, who from habit and prejudice would be unwilling to adopt a new method of teaching the language and a new pronunciation. Still there might be found some, and we trust there soon will be some, who will appreciate the many advantages of teaching the most beautiful language of antiquity as a living tongue. A teacher could in a few hours learn the pronunciation, and by reading a few modern books, and learning good dialogues, be enabled in a short time to make some progress in conversation.

To introduce this system fully and to make it a success, there should be an educated Greek attached to each of our public schools, to teach the pronunciation, to hear the pupils read aloud, and to converse with them. The critical elucidation of the language should remain, as at present, in the hands of the regular teachers, using the proper pronunciation.

We venture to think that such a reform in the teaching of Greek would much facilitate its acquisition, and render its study much more attractive to pupils, and add considerably to its utility; for those pupils who might never acquire any facility in reading the writings of the ancient dramatists, might still be able to make out the meaning of most of what they might find in a Greek newspaper or modern book, and if business or pleasure should take them to Greece or the Levant, they could with little difficulty make themselves understood to the Greeks with whom they came in contact. It might not be classical Greek altogether that they used, but we may say with Ampère, "En tout cas, il vaut mieux de parler le Grec comme un mendiant d'Athènes que comme un helléniste de Rotterdam."

With regard to learning Greek in this manner Professor Blackie says, "I undertake to prove that by learning Greek in the natural and true way as a living language, by a direct appeal to the ear and response by the tongue, thinking and speaking in Greek from the first lesson, a greater familiarity with that noble language will be acquired in five months than is done now by the assiduous labour of as many years. Nature is always right; schoolmasters and scholars are sometimes wrong." We hope that the learned and genial professor will not remain, what he has been for many years, with regard to this question, a " vox clamantis in deserto."

We may not have satisfied the critical demands, or removed all the difficulties, or even any from the minds of the advocates of the old system, but we trust we have shown sufficiently, that we have some basis for the view we have taken of Greek pronunciation. In conclusion we say with Cicero, " Ex filio locutum esse patrem judico, sic majores."

THE END.

www.ingramcontent.com/pod-product-compliance
Lightning Source LLC
Chambersburg PA
CBHW021524270326
41930CB00008B/1083